A LITTLE GOES A

long

WAY

52 DAYS TO A SIGNIFICANT LIFE

RACHAEL ADAMS

BroadStreet
PUBLISHING

BroadStreet Publishing® Group, LLC
Savage, Minnesota, USA
BroadStreetPublishing.com

A Little Goes a Long Way: 52 Days to a Significant Life
Copyright © 2022 Rachael Adams

978-1-4245-6449-1 (faux leather)
978-1-4245-6450-7 (e-book)

Stock or custom editions of BroadStreet Publishing titles may be purchased in bulk for educational, business, ministry, fundraising, or sales promotional use. For information, please email orders@broadstreetpublishing.com.

Author is represented by The Blythe Daniel Agency, Inc. | theblythedanielagency.com/

Cover and interior by Garborg Design Works | garborgdesign.com

Printed in China

22 23 24 25 26 5 4 3 2 1

Dedication

To Bryan, Will, and Kate. Thank you for your unconditional love and unwavering support. The little moments we share each day prove to me this message is true.

Contents

Welcome

"A little goes a long way" is a familiar saying we apply to all sorts of things—from spice, to garlic, to logic, to flattery, to perfume, to jewelry, to makeup, and on. But beyond our kitchens, closets, philosophies, and compliments, every little thing we do can go a long way in God's hands. I am learning that small things make a big difference, especially when we do them consistently over time.

We see this concept throughout the Bible in the lives of men and women who did something big with the little they were given. Joseph was the youngest in his family and was sold into slavery, but because of his faithfulness to God, he eventually rose to a position of power and saved the Egyptians and Israelites from famine. Gideon was the least of his family, yet his small army defeated the much larger Midianites. David was also the youngest of his family, but with just a sling and a stone, he defeated Goliath. Esther was an orphan placed in the king's palace, but she saved the Jewish people from annihilation and preserved Jesus' bloodline. And may we not forget Jesus himself, born in a manger in the middle of tiny Bethlehem, but grew up to save the entire world. God's greatest plan began with something small.

During Jesus' time on earth, he demonstrated the importance of "a little."

He valued the little things: hairs on our heads, birds in the air, and flowers in the field.

He noticed the little things: a slight touch of his garment, a diminutive tax collector perched in a tree, and a widow and her two coins. He served in little ways: washing feet, holding children, and cooking fish. He rewarded little deeds: the woman bathing his feet with her tears, the leper who said thank you, and the woman by the well who gave him something to drink.

Nothing was too insignificant for the Savior of the world. So why do we regularly consider bigger to be better? Friend, God sees and values every little thing you do. We can affect others while standing in the checkout line or sitting on the game field sidelines, while walking the dog or talking to a colleague at work. Believe it or not, when you partner with God, he can use even the most minute things to affect eternity in ways beyond what you can imagine. People like you and me can accomplish great things in our everyday moments by offering all we are and all we have to God.

Little things aren't little to him. We are making an eternal impact even when we don't see tangible results. I hope to help you believe this truth on our journey together.

This book will guide you through fifty-two devotions that you can read at your own pace—in one sitting, one a day, one a week, or sporadically throughout the year. You can read them in order or pick one that appeals to you at the moment—it truly is up to you. In each devotion, you will find personal stories coupled with Scripture. Also included is a little task for you to do and a personal prayer to say. To be clear, the goal isn't for you to do more but to trust in the value of all the little you are already doing.

If you are longing for significance and questioning whether your contributions matter, I pray that by the time you reach the end of this devotional, you will understand how important what you do is and how significant you truly are. A significant life is simpler (and smaller) than you think.

On the journey with you,
Rachael

A Little Beginning

"Do not despise these small beginnings,
for the LORD rejoices to see the work begin."
ZECHARIAH 4:10 NLT

I was born and raised in a small, rural Kentucky town. After going away to college and getting married, I returned to my hometown. I briefly worked outside the home until we had our children, at which point I decided to stay home with them full time. My days revolved around diapers, bottles, and Cheerios. Even though I knew in my heart it was important work, some days it didn't feel that way.

Both of my children are in school now, so most days I'm alone as I attend to my daily responsibilities, accompanied only by my animals. When my husband, Bryan, comes home from work and asks how my day was, I list all of the things I accomplished: I read my Bible, made the beds, walked the dogs, wrote a devotion, recorded a podcast, went to the grocery store, paid bills, cooked dinner, washed dishes and clothes, helped with homework, took the kids to their games, and so on. When he asks, he isn't necessarily asking what I've done, rather simply wondering how I am. Even knowing this, I still want the assurance that I'm doing a good job. That I am significant.

The thing is that this desire for assurance and significance is a daily occurrence. I lay my head down at night reflecting on what I've accomplished, and I wake up to my alarm and start again, back to what I perceive to be square one. Each day I have a choice.

Will I begin again regardless of how small my work seems in the grand scheme of things, trusting God is growing me and using it all? Or will I grow discouraged and be lulled to sleep by the monotony, believing it is all ineffective and pointless?

This is your choice too. While your to-do list may look different from mine, I have a feeling our hearts are similar. We want our lives to count, but we feel minuscule, like our ordinary, everyday moments will never amount to anything. We take stock of the families we were born into, the towns we grew up in, and the positions we serve in, then we determine they are of little value. If we aren't careful, we can start to believe that who we are, where we are, and what we are doing doesn't really matter.

A remnant of Jews who had returned to Judah to rebuild the temple and their nation had similar thoughts. Many of the older Jews were disheartened when they realized this new temple would not match the size and splendor of the previous temple built during King Solomon's reign.

But a minor prophet (not a major prophet, incidentally) named Zechariah gave the people encouragement from God by saying, "Do not despise these small beginnings, for the LORD rejoices to see the work begin" (4:10 NLT). The NIV translation says, "Who dares despise the day of small things." Zechariah was trying to communicate to them that bigger and more beautiful isn't always better. The presence of God on the inside of the temple was what made it significant.

Zechariah's fellow minor prophet Haggai says it this way, "How does it look to you now? Does it not seem to you like nothing?" (2:3). So often, who we are and what we are doing feels like nothing. But friend, because God is on the inside of us, we, too, are significant.

At the genesis of the world, God created us from dust (Genesis 2:7). With his breath, God brought life to something simple and small. He breathed life into us. He is the one who turns our ordinary lives into something extraordinary. In him, we have significance, and everything we do for him is meaningful. May we stop questioning the value of who we are and what we do, and may we accept that we are important to God's purpose in this generation. He rejoices in what is right not necessarily what is big. Be faithful in the small. Begin where you are, do what you can, and leave the results up to God. I pray we no longer seek or crave outside affirmation but settle in our minds and hearts that his validation is enough.

Today is a genesis of our own as we embark on this devotional journey of living with significance. Keep going and persevere to the end, celebrating tiny victories and growth all along the way.

Your Little Task

What is God asking you to begin or begin again? Start a record of the small steps you are taking toward your goal. Celebrate your progress and growth. Make note of each new milestone but remember that much of your growth will be on the inside. (He could simply be asking you to begin reading this devotional and complete these little tasks. If so, you can use the tracker in the back of the book to help with this process!)

Lord, help me to make peace with the little I am and the little I have. May I remember I am small compared to you and that it is your Spirit that breathes life into anything I do. Father, assure me that you rejoice when I begin. Give me the courage to begin and to celebrate the person that I am and the location where you have placed me. When I am tempted to quit, help me persevere. Remind me that although I start at the beginning, you have a beautiful ending in store. Amen.

A Little Love

> *"My command is this:*
> *Love each other as I have loved you."*
> JOHN 15:12

"Would you live with me in a cardboard box?" my boyfriend, now husband, Bryan, asked as we sat on the concrete steps of the university student center. "I need to know that I'm enough for you no matter what life brings." After an awkward moment of silence, I told him no.

At the time, I didn't truly understand his question. However, after weathering job changes, bank account dips, childbirths, health crises, and five house moves (including living in a RV), I now understand. It doesn't matter what we have or where we go. What matters is that we have each other.

I also now understand that when Bryan asked if I would live in a cardboard box with him, he was asking whether I would act out my love in the ways that count most; he wanted to know if my love was more than mere words. When times got tough, would I still stay by his side?

Bryan and I refer back to our cardboard-box moment quite often. It reminds us to avoid getting caught up in the stuff of life and instead to focus on tangible, practical ways of showing love for one another. It helps us put our words into action; it helps us get back to the basics. I wonder if we need to get back to the basics of action-based love when it comes to our relationship with God too.

When asked, "Of all the commandments, which is the most important?" (Mark 12:28), Jesus answered, "'Love the Lord your God with all your heart and with all your soul and with all your mind and with all your strength.' The second is this: 'Love your neighbor as yourself.' There is no commandment greater than these" (vv. 30–31).

Jesus' response summarized all of God's laws, reducing them two simple principles: love God and love others. Later, he simplified the command even further, "My command is this: Love each other as I have loved you" (John 15:12).

Jesus demonstrated this law with his life, loving us all the way to the cross. As he was a living example of God's love, we are now to be a living example of that love to others.

In the Gospel of John, Peter learned about this principle firsthand after he had disowned Jesus three times. It was a back-to-the-basics, cardboard-box moment for Peter. I imagine Peter sitting with Jesus along the shore as Jesus questioned Peter three times. Jesus asked, "Do you truly love me more than these?…Do you really love me?…Are you even my friend?" In my mind, I picture Peter looking intently at Jesus, wondering where he was going with this line of questioning, not completely understanding what he meant by the probing.

When Peter answered each question with "Yes, I love you," Jesus responded, "Feed my sheep" (John 21:17). In essence, Jesus was saying, "Show your love for me by loving mankind. Not just with words, but with tangible action so that I am revealed through you and others may come to know and love me too."

Now it's your turn to be on the hot seat. Envision yourself sitting with Jesus in a cardboard-box, back-to-the-basics moment of your own. Hold his gaze and listen as he asks you, "Do you truly love me? Do you really love me? Are you even my friend?" We don't have to stare into space searching for a satisfactory answer because we already have a better understanding of what he means. We can respond immediately with an emphatic *yes*! Not just a yes with our words but a yes with our actions as well.

Your Little Task

Settle in your heart that God is your first love and open your heart to receive his love. Without his love you have nothing of significance to give.

Prayer Prompt

Lord, you are my first love. Forgive me for loving you for what you give me rather than for who you are. I know you love me for who I am and not for what I can give you. Enable me to love others as you have loved me. Help me to find my way back to the basics. Fill me with your Spirit to love a lot with the little I have. Open my eyes to see how a little love can go a long way. Amen.

DAY 3

A Little Vessel

"Your servant has nothing there at all," she said,
"except a small jar of olive oil."
2 KINGS 4:2

I polled my podcast listeners about how much they felt they had to offer God and others. On a scale of one to ten, with one being nothing and ten being a lot, the average answer was a three. When asked if they believed their contribution mattered, 83 percent responded no. I had hypothesized this would be the case; however, these findings were even more startling than I presumed. Would your response be similar?

In 2 Kings 4, we meet a woman who also felt like she had little to offer. She was a widow, and a creditor was coming to take her two boys as slaves. In desperation, she cried out to the prophet Elisha for help. Elisha replied to her, "How can I help you? Tell me, what do you have in your house?"

"'Your servant has nothing there at all,' she said, 'except a small jar of olive oil'" (4:2). Elisha instructed her to ask her neighbors for empty jars and specifically told her not to ask for "just a few" (v. 3). Once she had gathered them, she was to shut the door of her house, pour the oil into all the jars, and put them to the side as each of them was filled. She did as he advised. Her sons continued to bring jars, and she kept pouring. When there were no more jars, the oil stopped flowing. She had so much oil she was able to pay her debts and live on what was left (vv. 4–7).

I wonder if God is asking us a question similar to what Elisha asked the widow. Could he be asking, "What do you have?" And if so, how often do we respond, "I *only* have _____," or "*Nothing* except _____." But what strikes me so profoundly about this story is that although the widow knew she had nothing with which to fill the jars, she gathered them anyway. The number of jars she gathered was an indication of her faith as evidenced by the flow of oil only stopping when she ran out of containers. The widow was abundantly blessed as a result of her active faith—not in herself but faith in God working through her.

God's provision was as large as the widow and her sons' faith and their willingness to obey. The same is true of us. We may only have a little "oil," but God's supply is more than enough to fill our empty vessels. As we allow him to fill us, we can fill the world's empty spaces by using what he has given us. When we offer all we have, no matter how small and inadequate it may seem, we can trust God to turn it into immeasurably more than we can ask or imagine (Ephesians 3:20).

Sometimes acting in faith may come naturally for us, and other times we may need to borrow our neighbor's faith like the widow borrowed her neighbor's vessels. But rest assured, God is working in you, and you are enough just as you are. If we polled him on whether we have anything of value to give, I think he would respond with a perfect ten.

Your Little Task

Turn your hands with your palms facing up to God. In this posture, pray for God to fill your empty vessel and commit to him that you will pour out what he's given you to fill others too.

Prayer Prompt

Lord, I know I am empty without you. Forgive me for the times I go to any other source to fill me. You are the only one who ever sustains. May I be a vessel for you and overflow so others may be filled by you too. Amen.

A Little Invitation

*"Come, you who are blessed by my Father; take your inheritance,
the kingdom prepared for you since the creation of the world."*

MATTHEW 25:34

As a new mom, I was afraid to go anywhere during the first year of
my son's life. I was nervous Will would cry or get sick, so it seemed
safer to just stay home. But I knew being secluded for such a long
time was not healthy, and after a year of isolation, I was longing
for relationship.

Despite my fears, I decided to attend Toddler Tales at the
local library. There, a woman greeted me and invited me to join
her later that week at a MOPS (Mothers of Preschoolers) gathering.
I accepted her invitation, and while I was at the MOPS meeting,
another woman invited me to attend a local church. I accepted her
invitation as well, and while at church, another woman invited me
to join her for a women's Bible study. This led to my family joining
the church, my children being baptized, and my being asked to
lead a Bible study. This in turn led to my love for Bible studies like
the one you are reading right now. Amazingly, I am where I am
today because of the power of a simple invitation.

Jesus knew the power of personal invitations, too, and often
extended them. He invited people to participate in various activities, including the following:

To rest: "Come to me, all you who are weary and burdened,
and I will give you rest" (Matthew 11:28).

To see: "'Come,' he replied, 'and you will see'" (John 1:39).

To drink: "Let anyone who is thirsty come to me and drink" (John 7:37).

To dine: "Come and have breakfast" (John 21:12).

To take up the cross: "If anyone would come after me, let him deny himself and take up his cross and follow me" (Matthew 16:24 ESV).

To renew: "Come with me by yourselves to a quiet place and get some rest" (Mark 6:31).

To be blessed: "Come, you who are blessed by my Father; take your inheritance, the kingdom prepared for you since the creation of the world" (Matthew 25:34).

Did you notice the caveat in each of these invitations? Come. Jesus calls us to come. He made this point vividly clear in the parable of the wedding banquet. In Matthew 22, Jesus said, "The kingdom of heaven is like a king who prepared a wedding banquet for his son. He sent his servants to those who had been invited to the banquet to tell them to come, but they refused to come" (22:2–3).

In this story, the king invited his guests by sending two invitations. The first asked the guests to attend the banquet; the second announced that it was ready. Each time, they rejected his invitation by making excuses—they couldn't attend because of work duties, family responsibilities, financial needs, and so on. Therefore, the master told his servant to invite others and make them come in so his house would be full (Luke 14:15–24).

I love his open invitation, don't you? We, too, are invited into a relationship with God, but it is up to us to accept the invitation. Like those in the parable who turned down the invitation to the banquet, we often resist or delay responding to God's invitation. Are you making excuses to avoid responding to God's call?

Friend, Jesus invites you to be with him forever in eternity. How will you RSVP? Who will be your plus one?

Your Little Task

Knowing how God can use a little invitation to make a significant impact, think about someone to whom you can extend an invitation. Who knows where it may lead?

Prayer Prompt

Jesus, thank you for the opportunity to fellowship and commune with you. May I extend the same invitation to people in my life and trust you with the outcome. Draw us all closer to you. Come, Lord Jesus, come. Amen.

Day 5

A Little Yes

*"I am the Lord's servant," Mary answered.
"May your word to me be fulfilled."*

LUKE 1:38

I met my husband, Bryan, on the first day of college. We were in the same orientation group, and I remember eyeing him from across the circle of freshmen as we played icebreaker games under an oak tree. Nearly four years later, on the night before my graduation, he got down on one knee under that same oak tree and asked if I would marry him. With tears in my eyes, I enthusiastically said yes!

After a year-long engagement, we stood under a church steeple in front of God, family, and friends. To have and to hold from this day forward, for better, for worse, for richer, for poorer, in sickness and in health, to love and to cherish, till death do us part—we said yes to all.

Though it was easy to say yes in that moment, it has proven to be more difficult to keep saying yes over the course of our married life. Not because I don't love Bryan but because my selfish, sinful nature gets in the way much more often than I'd like.

My Christian walk has mirrored my marriage. It was easy to say yes to God and begin a relationship with him. Saying yes to eternity in heaven, unconditional love, unlimited forgiveness, and unmerited grace wasn't a hard decision for me. Jesus did all the hard work. I simply had to receive and trust in what he promised. What has proven to be more difficult is to keep saying yes to him for the rest of my life. It's easier to say yes to God when things are going well and life is running smoothly. But when he asks me to do something uncomfortable or inconvenient, the yes may not come as enthusiastically as before. Yet, it is precisely during these times that our answers to God's call should be a resounding yes.

There are many biblical examples of people saying yes to God's call to action despite the personal sacrifice it would require, but the one person who stands out in my mind is Mary, the mother of Jesus. God chose her for one of the most important acts of obedience he has ever asked of anyone. She was just a young unmarried girl with a willing heart. Even though she risked being publicly ridiculed and rejected by her family and future husband, when Gabriel appeared and announced that she would conceive a child by the Holy Spirit, Mary responded, "I am the Lord's servant…May your word to me be fulfilled" (Luke 1:38). Her yes helped bring the Savior into the world. And aren't we so grateful?

Mary didn't stop with just one yes. After she said yes to the angel, she kept on saying yes to whatever God was doing in her life. She said yes to traveling to Bethlehem to give birth in a stable. She said yes to letting Jesus leave home to preach the good news. And, she said yes to the agony of letting him say a yes of his own and be crucified on the cross.

If we want to be used by God like Mary was, it's important we know his voice so that we can discern what his personal direction is for each of us. After all, what God asks me to do may be very different from what he asks you to do. Once we know what he is leading us to do, we simply have to trust that he has our best interests in mind and be willing to do what he asks even if we don't understand why at the time. Watch what a willing heart and a lifetime of yeses can do.

Your Little Task

If you have never said yes to God by putting your trust fully in Jesus, there is no better time than this very moment. To say yes, you can say a simple prayer like this: *Lord, I admit I am a sinner. I need and want your forgiveness. I accept your death as the penalty for my sin, and I recognize that your mercy and grace are gifts you offer to me because of your great love, not because of anything I have done. By faith, I receive you into my heart as the Son of God and as Savior and Lord of my life. From now on, help me live for you. In your precious name. Amen.*

If you have said yes to God as your Lord and Savior, ask him to reveal your next step of obedience. Then say yes.

Prayer Prompt

Lord, I give you my yes. I commit everything I have and everything I am to you. I surrender and submit to your will. I am willing to follow wherever your Spirit leads. Amen.

Day 6

A Little Encounter

Now he had to go through Samaria…Jesus, tired as he was from the journey, sat down by the well. It was about noon.
JOHN 4:4–6

My first job out of college was as a community liaison for the government. I was responsible for a large region, and I had a long list of contacts in various communities across the eastern part of the state. With so much to learn, I was assigned a veteran liaison, Emily, to train me for the first several months. Each day Emily and I spent a significant amount of time together in our rental car, traveling from city to city.

Though I didn't realize it initially, I was receiving much more than training for my new job. I looked up to Emily professionally, but before long, I also began to look up to her spiritually. She became the mentor I didn't know I needed. I had a daily passenger-seat view into the way she lived out her faith—her countenance, choices, and character consistently aligned with the Word. I quietly observed her listening to Christian music, bringing Scripture into conversation, sharing godly wisdom, praying before meals, working hard, and loving people. While I had a salvation moment as a preteen, Emily opened my eyes to what having an active relationship with God actually meant. She helped me to realize I could encounter him personally each day, not just in eternity.

Eventually, the time came when I had to start traveling without Emily, but I now had the assurance of a new companion.

God took the driver's seat, and I joyfully remained in the passenger seat. Slowly, the behavior Emily had modeled became my behavior. Over time, I, too, found myself listening to Christian music, bringing Scripture into conversation, sharing godly wisdom, praying before meals, working hard, and loving people. I'm so grateful for this encounter with her during that season of my life. Though Emily likely didn't realize the positive impact she had on me when our lives intersected, God certainly knew what he was doing when he placed us together for those few months. He knew how much I needed her example.

As I reflect on this experience, I'm struck by the fact that, because my encounter with Emily changed me, all the people I've encountered since that training nearly two decades ago have also been affected. Many people have been touched because she was an ambassador of Jesus' love—and an encounter with Jesus changes everything.

This was certainly the case for the woman at the well. This woman is never named, yet her encounter with the Son of God is the longest exchange Jesus had with an individual in the Gospel of John (4:1–42). The story begins with Jesus traveling through Samaria on the way to Galilee. Tired from his journey, he sat down at a well in the town of Sychar. Most Jews avoided this city, but Jesus purposefully traveled there to encounter this woman who represented the lowest of the low—a female in a society where women were both demeaned and disregarded, a member of a race traditionally despised by the Jews, and a social outcast living in shame because of her lifestyle.

This woman came to draw water during the heat of the day, likely because she was trying to avoid encounters with other people due to her situation. How divine that she had a holy encounter with Christ instead. It's no coincidence Jesus was there at the exact place and exact time.

During their interaction, he asked her for a drink, and by the end of the conversation, Jesus had given her living water. The Samaritan woman gave him well water, but she gained so much more. Though she didn't initially understand the magnitude of this little encounter, she experienced the eternal effects. Jesus did more than satisfy her physical thirst; he also satisfied the spiritual thirst she didn't even realize she had. After this single encounter with Jesus, she led many more Samaritans from that town to encounter him and believe.

It is astounding to consider how many encounters we have on any given day. It is even more astounding to think about the potential significance each of those encounters can have. Whether these occurrences are scheduled or by surprise, frequent or rare, ongoing or once in a lifetime—God uses them all. What if we viewed every encounter as a divine appointment from him with the purpose of leading one another closer to him? Could your next encounter change the trajectory of your life, the other person's life, or both? May every encounter with you be an encounter with him. How exciting to someday see where those encounters will lead no matter how insignificant they may seem at the time.

Your Little Task

View the next encounter you have with a person as one that has the potential to change everything! Consider how an encounter with you could lead to the other person having an encounter with Christ.

Lord, thank you for the people you have placed in my life. I choose to believe every encounter is ordained and designed by you. Help me to realize that because I have encountered you, everyone I meet is an opportunity to share your love and good news. Use me in every interaction to allow others to experience you through me. Amen.

A Little Presence

"Never will I leave you;
never will I forsake you."
HEBREWS 13:5

A friend of mine had just returned from a long stay in the hospital with her son. As Robin spoke about her experience, she recalled how others had loved her well through cards, prayers, flowers, and meals. As I listened, I noticed Robin spent the most time reminiscing over the friend who had come to the hospital to just be with her. At that moment, I regretted that I hadn't taken the time to be present with her too.

Looking back, I realized I was afraid of imposing or saying the wrong thing, making her situation worse rather than better. I allowed myself to be paralyzed by fear, so I did nothing. Thinking about this interaction made me wonder if, when we encounter the needs of others, offering God's love isn't necessarily about finding the perfect gift or Bible verse. Rather, could offering our presence be one of the most significant things we do for one another?

In the Old Testament, God models the ministry of presence. From the very beginning, God said, "I am with you" (Genesis 28:15). From his presence in the burning bush to his presence in the tabernacle, we see evidence of God stepping into the realm of the human experience to minister to the needs of his people.

In the New Testament, God's love became physically present through Jesus. The Word literally became flesh and dwelt among us (John 1:14). His very name Immanuel means "God with us."

When we think about how we can be present in the lives of others, we need to look no further than the life of Jesus. He showed up to eat meals in homes, to bring peace in the midst of storms, to celebrate weddings, and to mourn side by side with friends.

Knowing our need for his presence, after Jesus left earth, he sent us the Holy Spirit. Presence can be our ministry because he is present in us. Spending time in God's presence allows our presence to be the gift he intends it to be for others. All we have to do is show up—no special skill or talent required.

One day, the presence of God will be even more intimate and precious than what we have already experienced on earth. This hope of eternity with God is the greatest comfort imaginable. I long for this kind of nearness to God, but until then, we can share his Spirit with each other in our daily lives.

Your Little Task

It's possible to be present in the body but not present in mind and heart. When you are with others, make sure you give them your full attention.

Prayer Prompt

Lord, thank you for being present to me and for your Spirit within me. Help me to follow your example of being present in the lives of others. Give me the strength to bear their burdens, weep when they weep, and rejoice when they rejoice until the day when we can all be in your presence eternally. Amen.

A Little Group

The Lord did not set his affection on you and choose you because
you were more numerous than other peoples, for you were the fewest
of all peoples.

DEUTERONOMY 7:7

I attended my first women's Bible study when I was in middle
school, and because of my age and spiritual immaturity, I felt out
of place. I didn't understand the Christian terms that seemed so
familiar to everyone else in attendance, and I listened in bewil-
derment to what sounded like a foreign language. My lack of
comprehension was evidenced by my failure to complete the
study—preteen me only completed two lessons.

Years later, a friend invited me to another Bible study.
I hadn't attended a group study since the one I attempted as a
preteen. While I still had to look at the table of contents to find
each book of the Bible, I finished the study this time. Being older
helped, but being surrounded by a community of women who
could answer my questions and with whom I could discuss God's
Word helped even more.

This small group of women became more than a means to
finish a Bible study. They challenged me, held me accountable, and
accepted me, flaws and all. This group of women gathered each
week, strengthened our respective family units, and launched service projects and other ministries in our community. This group
was so meaningful that we didn't stop after one Bible study—we've
been meeting now for years. It's been amazing to watch God grow

our group—not just in number but also in impact. And it all started with a few women who met consistently for an hour each Wednesday night.

It's easy to question whether a small group of people can make a big difference, but my experience proves otherwise—and so does the Bible. In fact, God told the Israelites that he didn't choose them because they were the most numerous group but, rather, because they were the fewest (Deuteronomy 7:7). They were not God's chosen people because of their merit but because of his promise to their ancestors. When their forerunners entered Egypt, they were a small family group of seventy people, but in time, they grew to become a nation with a population as numerous as the stars in the sky or the grains of sand on the seashore (Deuteronomy 10:22).

Gideon's story is another example of the power of small groups. His clan was the weakest in Manasseh, and he was the least in his family (Judges 6:15). When God asked him to go into battle against the Midianites, Gideon struggled to believe that he and his army could win. But God promised to be with them. As they prepared for battle, God decreased the odds of victory even more, telling Gideon he had too many men. He reduced their soldiers from thirty-two hundred to three hundred! Remarkably, Gideon's small army routed thousands of Midianites without a single man drawing a sword. With an army so outnumbered, there could be no doubt the victory was from God.

Just as God used small groups of people in the Old Testament, Jesus used small groups of people in the New Testament. He frequently ministered to thousands, but he always returned to the same small group of twelve disciples. Then, after his death and resurrection, that little group of disciples took his message from their home city of Jerusalem to Judea, to Samaria, and to the ends of the earth

(Acts 1:8). Empowered by the Holy Spirit, the early church emerged from this small group of believers.

What these early believers started, we must continue. As was the case for the Israelites, Gideon's army, and the disciples, we can't accomplish anything in our own strength or by our own merit. Only when God is a part of the equation will these little groups increase in number and impact the world. The good news for us is that Jesus promised that where two or three come together in his name, he would be with them (Matthew 18:20). Friend, it is not about the size of the group God has given you, rather it is the magnitude of the One within you.

Your Little Task

Consider joining a small group through your church. Watch how God uses the group of believers to further his kingdom for his glory.

Prayer Prompt

Lord, give me a group of believers to experience life with. Help me to recognize the value of the people you have already given me. I don't ever want the group to be exclusive. Lead me to include or be included wherever you want me. Remind me it is your presence in me and within the group that allows us to make any lasting impact. Amen.

DAY 9

A Little Belief

"Everything is possible
for one who believes."
MARK 9:23

"If you could see yourself through my eyes, it would change your world," my husband, Bryan, told me years ago. I honestly don't remember the circumstances surrounding his profound statement, but I imagine it was another conversation in which he was trying to help me believe in myself.

Insecurity has been the thorn in my side for as long as I can remember. But, because of my loved one's belief in me, I've taken steps of faith I never dreamed I would. One of the things I never would have believed I'd do is be a podcast host.

To give you a better understanding of why this reality seemed so far-fetched, let me share a bit more of my background. In college, I thought I wanted to major in broadcast journalism. I dreamed of being the next Katie Couric from the *Today Show*. During my freshman year, one of the prerequisites was a public speaking class. For my final exam, I had to present a persuasive speech in front of the class. While I don't remember the grade I received (probably because I wanted to forget it), I do remember the anxiety I experienced. So much so, I dropped the major in defeat and switched to business management. Fast forward to my life now, communicating to the public through both written and spoken form is the majority of what I do on a daily basis. How ironic, right?

Even though it is out of my comfort zone, interviewing women for my podcast has become one of God's greatest gifts to me. I love getting to know and learn from so many incredible women. In one of the interviews, I was chatting with a *New York Times* bestselling author about her writing journey. During our conversation, she mentioned that, growing up, her dad always told her, "Someone has to be the next *New York Times* bestselling author. It might as well be you." Is it a coincidence that she achieved what her father believed she could do? I don't think so, because belief in others can be a powerful thing.

A prime example of the impact of belief in the life of another is seen through Barnabas' relationship with Saul in the book of Acts. Before Saul's Damascus-road moment, he had spent his life persecuting Christians. Because of his history, the disciples doubted Saul's conversion and were afraid of him. But Barnabas believed in Saul and became a bridge between him and the apostles. As a result, Saul became Paul. He was transformed from a persecutor of Christians to a preacher for Christ, and he went on to preach throughout the Roman empire on three missionary journeys. Paul wrote letters to various churches, which eventually became part of the New Testament. Paul's belief in Christ was the primary source of his transformation, but Barnabas' belief in him also played a significant part.

Could your belief in someone change their world? Moreover, could it change *the* world? I believe so! When a person encourages you to believe in yourself the possibilities are endless. Imagine the Lord saying, "Daughter, if you could only see yourself through my eyes, it would change your world." Our belief in him and his presence in us changes our belief in ourselves. Once we have this confidence, it is essential we help others believe in him and understand how that belief makes everything else possible (Mark 9:23).

Your Little Task

Think about someone in your life who might be struggling to believe in Christ, believe in themselves, or both. How can you come alongside to encourage them to believe?

Prayer Prompt

Lord, help me to believe in you and to trust in the ways you have uniquely gifted me. Show me how I can encourage someone else to believe in you and have faith in themselves. Father, I want to believe; help my unbelief. Amen.

A Little Preparation

*"My Father's house has many rooms; if that were not so, would I
have told you that I am going there to prepare a place for you?
And if I go and prepare a place for you, I will come back and take
you to be with me that you also may be where I am."*

JOHN 14:2–3

A friend of mine is a baker and sugar artist. Chrissy's creations not
only look beautiful, but they also taste delicious. One day in her
kitchen, I noticed she was gathering all her tools and prepping her
ingredients. When I asked about her process, she explained it was
called *mise en place*, a French culinary phrase that means "putting
in place." It refers to the setup of ingredients and tools required
before cooking or baking. Essentially, it is the process of preparing.

After learning about *mise en place*, I was thinking about
how God is preparing us and putting everything in its place in our
lives. We see how this transpired with the characters in the Bible,
even though their "preparation" was typically unbeknownst to
them while they were in the midst of it.

Moses, for example, was adopted into a royal Egyptian
family and later lived as a nomad shepherd. Little did he know,
this training was preparation for the last forty years of his life. God
used these experiences to train him to lead the Israelites through
the desert (Exodus).

Because Moses understood the value of preparation, it is no
surprise that he began training Joshua to be his aide. Joshua played
a key role in the exodus from Egypt, acted as the field general

of Israel's army, accompanied Moses partway up the mountain when he received the law, and scouted the promised land. All of these exploits helped him to lead the Israelites after Moses' death (Joshua 3).

Like these men, our preparation begins at an early age. Our whole lives are God's training ground. He uses a variety of means to develop us: hereditary traits, environmental influences, and personal experiences. However, we can also prepare ourselves for whatever lies ahead by reading our Bible, worshiping, and praying.

God is putting everything in its place for your future, and we can aid him in this process. What can you do today to better prepare for tomorrow? Stay close to God so when he calls you to a task, you can be confident that you have the tools needed for what's ahead.

Your Little Task

Reflect on how God has prepared you for your current season. What can you do to better prepare for the season ahead?

Prayer Prompt

Lord, I praise you for your providence and sovereignty. I am grateful for the ways you have been training me throughout my life. Help me to take responsibility to prepare myself so I am ready for the opportunities and trials that come my way. Thank you for preparing a place for me forever with you. Amen.

A Little Meal

They devoted themselves to the apostles' teaching and to fellowship,
to the breaking of bread, and to prayer.

When I came home from the hospital after having Will and then again after having Kate, some of the biggest blessings I received were the meals brought to us by friends and family. Being sleep-deprived and adjusting to life with a newborn, the last thing I wanted to do was think about what to make for dinner.

Although it was years ago, I still remember my next-door neighbor, Hilary, bringing over meatballs and sides for dinner. The meatballs were such a hit with my family that I asked her for the recipe. Since then, this meal has become a regular part of my cooking rotation as evidenced by the worn appearance of the recipe card. In fact, now when a friend has a new baby or has surgery, I take them this same dish. It's easy to double, so my family is fed simultaneously too.

My neighbor's gesture affected more than just my hunger. Her gesture also fed my soul. I'm willing to bet that you have sweet memories that involve a meal too. Food has a way of feeding us not only physically but also spiritually, doesn't it?

Throughout the Bible, we find many examples of the significance of a little meal. One notable meal mentioned in Scripture is the Passover. This meal commemorated the night the Israelites were freed from Egypt (Exodus 12). A seven-day festival called the Feast of Unleavened Bread followed Passover. This, too, recalled the Israelites' quick escape from Egypt when they didn't have time to let their bread rise.

Jesus shared many meals too. Bread and fish seem to be his favorite dishes. We read about him reclining at tables and hosting dinner parties along the shoreline. He had intimate gatherings with seven for breakfast (John 21) and with twelve at the last supper (Matthew 26). He also held larger gatherings, feeding crowds of five thousand (Mark 6) and four thousand (Mark 8) with a few fish and bread that he multiplied! Reading these examples from Jesus' life serves to confirm for me that he is concerned with every aspect of our lives—the physical as well as the spiritual.

Following suit, the early church also valued mealtime together. The book of Acts tells us "They devoted themselves to the apostles' teaching and to fellowship, to the breaking of bread and to prayer" (2:42).

Today we can fellowship the same way. Meals shared around the table are how we connect, remember, celebrate, and mourn. We don't have to be gourmet cooks to make a meaningful impact. Store-bought dinner or restaurant takeout can be equally as thoughtful, helpful, and memorable as homemade because the significance of a meal lies not in the food but in the people and the conversations we have. Whether it's simple or extravagant, a meal can go a long way toward growing the bonds of love between family and friends.

PS: The meatball recipe is in the appendix (A Little Flavor).

Your Little Task

What is your favorite meal? Invite someone to share it with you.

Lord, thank you for being the Bread of Life and my daily bread. I am grateful for the food you have created and continue to provide for me. Thank you for sustaining and nourishing me physically and spiritually. Take my little offering of food and use it to go a long way in my relationships and in the stomachs and hearts of others. Amen.

A Little Walk

*A Samaritan, as he traveled, came where the man was;
and when he saw him, he took pity on him.*

LUKE 10:33

My dogs and I take a walk most days. Usually, I walk the
cross-country course on our farm that follows the fence rows and
cuts through the woods, but before we moved to the farm, I used
to walk around the neighborhood we lived in. Though I usually
traveled the surrounding roads by myself, using the time to think
and talk to the Lord, I often ended up passing a neighbor in their
yard or out for a walk of their own.

On one particular walk, I happened upon a close friend.
As we were catching up and talking about life, I mentioned I
would be attending a writers' conference the following month.
Unbeknownst to me at the time, this friend also wanted to write
books. I nonchalantly invited Trudy to attend with me, telling her
I had an extra spot for her in my car and my hotel room if she
wanted to go. I never thought she would actually take me up on
my offer, but soon after we parted ways, I received a text from her
that said, "I'm in!"

Fast forward three years, Trudy has published two books,
and she'll probably publish more. She says all the time, "If it wasn't
for bumping into you on that walk, I wouldn't be where I am now."
While I know God can use many people and resources to lead us
and encourage us, it does make me smile to think I might have

played a small part in her story. I imagine you've had your own unexpected moments on a simple walk as well.

As I think about how Jesus connected with others, I realize he often connected with people while he was walking along roads. He also featured this in his parables, such as in the parable of the good Samaritan. In the story, a man was traveling on the road from Jerusalem to Jericho when he fell into the hands of robbers. They stripped him of his clothes, beat him, and went away, leaving him half dead. A priest happened to be going down the same road, and when he saw the man, he passed by on the other side. So too, a Levite, when he came to the place and saw him, passed by on the other side. But a Samaritan, as he traveled, came to where the man was, and when he saw him, he took pity on him. He went to him and bandaged his wounds, pouring on oil and wine. Then he put the man on his own donkey, brought him to an inn, and took care of him. The next day he took out two denarii and gave them to the innkeeper. "'Look after him,' he said, 'and when I return, I will reimburse you for any extra expense you may have'" (Luke 10:35).

Jesus told this parable in response to a man's question: "Who is my neighbor?" (Luke 10:29). The man, who was an expert in the law, treated the wounded man as a topic for discussion; the robbers in the story treated the wounded man as an object to exploit; the priest treated the man as a problem to avoid; the Levite treated him as an object of curiosity; and the innkeeper treated him as a customer to serve for a fee. Only the Samaritan treated the injured man as a person to love.

Keep in mind, the Jews considered themselves to be pure descendants of Abraham and considered the Samaritans to be a mixed-race because they had intermarried after Israel's exile. As a result, there was deep hatred between the two groups. Knowing this background sheds light onto why this Samaritan's actions were considered so good. It also sheds light on who our neighbor is and what it means to be a good neighbor. Our neighbor is anyone of any race, creed, or social background. If we see a neighbor with a need, whether physical, financial, emotional, or spiritual, being loving means acting to meet that need. Jesus praised the good Samaritan's actions and told us to, "Go and do likewise" (Luke 10:37). Who will you encounter as you walk along during your day? May you view them as a person to love.

Your Little Task

Take a walk and pay attention to the people you pass. Ask God to give you the opportunity to be a good Samaritan.

Prayer Prompt

Lord, whether I turn to the right or to the left, may I hear your voice saying, "'This is the way; walk in it'" (Isaiah 30:21). No matter where I go and whom I meet along the road, help me to see each individual as a person to love and as an opportunity to fulfill your command to love my neighbor as myself. Amen.

A Little Dream

"When there is a prophet among you, I, the LORD,
reveal myself to them in visions, I speak to them in dreams."
NUMBERS 12:6

What did you dream about as a little girl? When I was younger, I dreamed of being an actress in a movie or a singer on stage. I dreamed of prince charming arriving on a white horse to marry me like in all the fairy tales. I would play house with my baby powder–scented Cabbage Patch dolls and dream of being a mother one day. Other days, I would sit on my window seat with a sketchbook on my lap and paint the neighbor's house in watercolors while dreaming of a home of my own.

Some of these childhood dreams have come to fruition, and others have not—not yet at least. I'm willing to bet the same is true of you. It seemed easier to dream back then, didn't it? Perhaps because we had bigger imaginations and were less jaded by life experience. But dreams do still come true and not just at Disney amusement parks or at night while we are fast asleep.

I believe God gives us visions and desires for our lives—glimpses of our potential future realities (Numbers 12:6). While we may not consider ourselves modern-day prophets, I've always heard there is some validity to the idea that what you dreamed about as a child is an indicator of what your future should be. I wonder if we have given up on many of our dreams too soon.

I remember a pivotal moment for me as a writer was when a literary agent said one of the biggest mistakes she sees aspiring authors make is they stop writing after receiving a rejection or correction. Could the same statement be made for many of our dreams? We meet a roadblock or encounter a detour that seems to be taking far too long, so we presume it "isn't meant to be."

God spoke to many of our spiritual forefathers through dreams, visions, and prophecies. Through their lives, we see that, often, the fulfillment of the dream did not come easily but rather required persistence and action.

One of the most notable Old Testament dreamers is Joseph (Genesis 37–50). At the age of seventeen, he had two dreams. The first involved sheaves of grain, which represented his brothers, bowing down to him. In the second dream, the sun, the moon, and eleven stars, which symbolized his father, mother, and brothers, bowed down to him. Thirteen years later, after being rejected and sold into slavery by his family, imprisoned, and then eventually promoted to second-in-command in Egypt, Joseph's dreams finally became reality. While he may have not chosen all that transpired in his life leading up to his dreams coming to fruition, in retrospect, he believed God used it all for good to save many lives throughout Egypt.

Did you notice Joseph's dreams weren't just about him? Our dreams aren't only about us either. God gives them to us for the benefit of others and for the furthering of his kingdom. When we dream, we should consider: If this became a reality, would it please God? If our dreams line up with Scripture, are consistent with his character, and will require his activity to transpire, then they are most likely from him.

While our dreams might not be as vivid or clear as those described in biblical times, if we get quiet with the Lord, we can ask him to reveal the dreams he has for our lives. Sometimes those dreams will come in the night, and sometimes he'll implant them in our hearts during our waking hours. Either way, just like in the lives of these heroes of our faith, our dreams will one day come true even if they don't happen in the way or in the time that we think they should.

How do I know? You're holding one of my dreams in your hands right now. Sweet dreams, sister.

Your Little Task

Let's take a note from Martin Luther King Jr. and his famous, history-changing "I Have a Dream" speech. After praying and spending time with God, finish this sentence: "I have a dream to..."

Prayer Prompt

Lord, thank you for speaking to me in all the ways you do. Remind me of the dreams I have forgotten or tried to forget. Show me new aspirations that not only benefit me but also others. May I be resilient and persevere to keep dreaming, even when it takes longer or is harder than I think it should be. And help me support others in the dreams you have given them. Amen.

A Little Perspective

*And Elisha prayed, "Open his eyes, LORD, so that he may see."
Then the LORD opened the servant's eyes, and he looked and saw
the hills full of horses and chariots of fire all around Elisha.*

2 KINGS 6:17

"Are we making any progress?" I asked my daughter, Kate, from my seated position inside the middle of the hole. My family was enjoying a day at the beach, and while my husband and son played catch, Kate and I decided to dig a hole big enough for both of us to fit in. We had been shoveling for quite a while, and from my vantage point, it didn't look like we had accomplished much. But from the outside looking in, Kate had a much different perspective. "We are, Mom! You just can't see it from where you are."

Doesn't life feel this way sometimes? We consider how hard we've been working and then look around in disappointment, thinking we should be further along by now. Negative thoughts crowd our minds, digging a dark hole of their own. *Why is this taking so long? Why isn't my hard work paying off?*

Our earthly perspective is limited, and the truth is that there is so much going on behind the scenes that we aren't aware of. This reality is vividly revealed through the story of Elisha and his servant found in 2 Kings 6. In the midst of a battle, the servant was scared at the sight of the physical army surrounding them. Recognizing his fear, Elisha prayed, "Open his eyes, Lord, so that he may see." God opened the servant's eyes to the spiritual realm, at which point he could see that a mighty heavenly army—much bigger than the physical army—was surrounding them too (6:8–23).

I take great comfort knowing there is a mighty heavenly army surrounding us as well. While we may not be in a literal battle, we are all battling our own set of difficult circumstances. We, too, can pray for eyes of faith to see God's perspective in the midst of what we are going through. We can keep working and trust we are further along than our vantage point allows us to see. God sees the complete picture while we only have snapshots. He is omniscient and omnipresent, so when we cry out to him, "Are we making any progress, Lord? Are you with me in this?" I imagine him responding, "Yes! You just can't see it from where you are." To which we pray like Elisha, "Lord, open my eyes to see."

Your Little Task

Offer someone your outside perspective. They may be struggling to recognize how much they are accomplishing or to see God's presence in their present situation. Help them to see themselves the way God sees them.

Prayer Prompt

*Lord, give me your eyes to see my circumstance
and the people in my life through your perspective.
Help me to be farsighted rather than nearsighted.
Shift my focus from earthly to eternal. Open my
eyes to see you everywhere and in everything.
Amen.*

A Little Work

Whatever you do, work at it with all your heart, as working for the Lord, not for human masters, since you know that you will receive an inheritance from the Lord as a reward. It is the Lord Christ you are serving.

COLOSSIANS 3:23–24

Do you ever think that the work you do doesn't matter? I have been guilty of believing this lie. Most days, I have my fingers on a computer writing or my mouth near a microphone podcasting. Other times, I am running errands, folding laundry, cooking meals, making beds, washing dishes, and helping with homework. Yet, despite all I accomplish, when people ask me what I do, I respond that I'm *just* a mom or *just* a writer.

Like me, many of us are quick to downplay the importance of the work we do, but the reality is that God values and uses our work—no matter what profession (or lack thereof) we have.

Since creation, God has given us work to do. It began with Adam when he was first put in the garden of Eden to work it and take care of it (Genesis 2:15). Later he was banned from the garden of Eden as a result of his disobedience. God cursed the ground and promised that Adam would only eat of it through painful toil and by the sweat of his brow. We've been toiling ever since, but God promises our "labor in the Lord is not in vain" (1 Corinthians 15:58). The key words here are "in the Lord." It is God who makes our work meaningful when we devote it to him.

Let's look at some biblical examples of the various jobs God used. He used a political leader named Joseph to save his family from famine (Genesis 39), a shepherd named Moses to lead Israel out of bondage and into the promised land (Exodus 3), a farmer named Gideon to deliver Israel from Midian (Judges 6), a homemaker named Hannah to be the mother of the prophet Samuel (1 Samuel 1), a shepherd boy named David to be Israel's greatest king (1 Samuel 16), a scribe named Ezra to lead the return to Judah and to write some of the Bible (Ezra), a slave girl named Esther to save her people from massacre (Esther), a peasant girl named Mary to be the mother of Christ (Luke 1), a tax collector named Matthew to be an apostle and Gospel writer (Matthew 9), a physician named Luke to be a companion of Paul and a Gospel writer (Colossians 4), and a fisherman named Peter to be an apostle, a leader of the early church, and writer of two New Testament letters (Matthew 4).

I imagine each of these individuals had days that felt menial and tiring, but they continued working faithfully at whatever task God placed before them. If God used all of these people in the midst of their ordinary work in such mighty ways, he can certainly use what you do in mighty ways too.

Scripture tells us that whatever we do, we should do with all our heart because it is the Lord we are serving (Colossians 3:23–24). This mindset shift helps me tremendously. When our assignments feel mundane or the fruit of our labor doesn't seem evident, it is important to adjust our perspective so that we see our work as another way to serve God. Ultimately, this means doing our daily work out of love for him.

Your Little Task

Ask God to reveal the kingdom impact of your daily jobs and chores. No matter what work you do, pray God helps you realize your significant contribution.

Prayer Prompt

Lord, thank you for giving me your work to do in the world. Help me to view everything I do as an opportunity to serve your holy work. Give me a new sense of purpose for each job and show me the fruit of my labor. Help me see how each task can glorify you and yield eternal results. Amen.

A Little Song

Sing to the LORD a new song;
sing to the LORD, all the earth.
PSALM 96:1

In a previous devotion, I mentioned one of my dreams as a young girl was to be a recording artist. Without reservation, I would belt out the lyrics to my favorite songs whether I really knew the words or not! On many occasions, I'd choreograph dance moves to coincide, too, but can I let you in on a little secret? Singing on a stage is not in my future (except maybe in a really large choir to drown out my voice) because I don't have a musical bone in my body. I have a terrible singing voice and zero rhythm. I can't even clap to the right beat!

Regardless of my lack of musical ability, I still love music. I think it's remarkable how hearing a song from the past can conjure the memory of where we were and what we were doing when we last heard it. We can easily remember lyrics to songs but can't remember our email password or where we left our keys.

There is something special about music. It has a unique way of staying with us and speaking straight to our souls. Have you ever heard a song on the radio or at church that was exactly what you needed to hear? I certainly have. I've even noticed whatever I've been listening to the previous day is what I wake up singing the next morning or humming throughout the day. Before I know it, the people around me start humming and singing along too. A simple song can have powerful effects.

In the Bible, we witness the impact of a song in the life of the missionaries Paul and Silas. They were stripped, beaten, and placed in jail for preaching the gospel. Despite their dismal situation, they praised God through prayer and song as the other prisoners listened. Suddenly, a violent earthquake shook the foundations of the prison and broke the prisoners' chains. In response to the commotion, the jailer cried out in fear and asked, "What must I do to be saved?" (Acts 16:30). The jailer's question opened up the opportunity for Paul and Silas to lead him and his entire household to the Lord.

We also see the power of song through the life of David. He was gifted musically and wrote the majority of the Psalms, which is the largest collection of songs in the Bible. His melodies express the whole range of the human experience—from depths of despair to heights of celebration.

While we are still influenced by his recorded lyrics today, we see an immediate effect of his music in the life of King Saul who was being tormented by an evil spirit. Searching for relief, Saul's attendants sent for David to play the harp for him. When David played, the evil spirit left Saul, and he felt better (1 Samuel 16:23). David's music brought an atmosphere of peace. Our songs of worship can change the entire atmosphere for us too. Whether you are musically inclined or not, lift your voice or listen to worship music and watch what God can do.

Your Little Task

Make intentional choices to turn on worship music today. Sing along in praise to the Lord.

Prayer Prompt

Lord, thank you for taking delight in me and for rejoicing over me with singing. Help me to stay in harmony with you. Put a new song in my heart and on my lips so others may sing of your praises too. Amen.

A Little Companionship

Ruth replied, "Don't urge me to leave you or to turn back from you.
Where you go I will go, and where you stay I will stay. Your people
will be my people and your God will be my God."

RUTH 1:16

"I left my window open hoping someone would come by to visit," Bryan's grandmother remarked. On a recent visit to her nursing home, my family and I huddled on the lawn outside her window while she sat inside, behind the glass. Due to the restrictions from the pandemic, visitors were not allowed inside, nor was she allowed to leave without being quarantined for several weeks afterward. We understood the restrictions, but it didn't lessen our feelings of helplessness or the loneliness she felt, especially since her husband had recently passed away.

You see, she doesn't have to be in a nursing home. Her body and her mind are healthy, but she chose to enter the home to be with her husband of seventy years who did need the medical help. While she could no longer care for him in the way she needed to medically, she was there with him emotionally. Every day, she was present with him as a hand to hold, an ear to listen, and a companion to provide comfort. Now that her husband has passed, our family tries to offer the company she needs.

Our interaction that day made me pause to consider how many other residents were sitting by their window in hopes of a visitor. Even beyond the nursing home, how many other people in our world are longing for someone to stop by and stay awhile to visit? I imagine more people than we will ever realize are lonely and waiting for companionship.

The book of Ruth tells a beautiful story of companionship. A widowed woman by the name of Naomi was left without her two sons and her husband. Upon their deaths, Naomi decided to return home to Israel. She took her two daughters-in-law, Orpah and Ruth, with her, but partway down the road, she selflessly told them to go back to their homeland. Orpah kissed Naomi good-bye and returned home, but Ruth loyally clung to her and said, "Don't urge me to leave you or to turn back from you. Where you go I will go, and where you stay I will stay. Your people will be my people and your God will be my God" (Ruth 1:16).

Ruth didn't just say these words; she meant them. The two women traveled together to Bethlehem and gleaned from the fields. They shared deep sorrow, great affection for one another, and, most importantly, a commitment to the Lord. In the succeeding months, God led Ruth to a man named Boaz, whom she eventually married. As a result, she became the great-grandmother of David and an ancestor in the line of the Messiah. The relationship between these women made such a profound impact!

Our relationships can also have profound impact. We need each other, yet so many of us are lonely. While people may not be literally cracking open the window of their home in hopes of a visitor, could they be cracking open the window of their hearts in hopes of someone seeing them? Could the mom standing alone on the edge of the playground while her kids play be secretly wishing for a friend to talk to? Might the neighbor who spends the afternoon sitting on her porch welcome a cup of tea and some conversation?

If you, dear friend, are the lonely one, I would encourage you to crack open the window of your heart. I pray someone in your life sees it and comes for a visit. If they don't, I pray you are bold enough to visit the window of another person and extend the invitation for companionship first.

And of course, in the event that you are still sitting alone by your window, you can rest assured that you are never truly alone. The Lord is ever-present and the best companion of all.

Your Little Task

Do you know someone who might be lonely and in need of companionship? Go and simply spend time with them.

Prayer Prompt

Father, thank you for being my constant companion. You are my best friend forever. I am grateful for the relationships you have given me. Help me to be a loyal and dependable friend. Soften my heart and make me aware of people who are longing for companionship. Give me boldness to reach out and be the friend they need. Amen.

A Little Celebration

In a loud voice, she exclaimed: "Blessed are you among women, and blessed is the child you will bear! But why am I so favored, that the mother of my Lord should come to me?"

LUKE 1:42–43

I was flipping through Will's yearbook from the previous school year when I came across a photograph of him from football season. The picture showed one of his coaches lifting him off the ground in a big hug while his teammates and the other coaches surrounded them, celebrating Will's interception. It was the State Championship game, and he had intercepted a touchdown pass late in the fourth quarter. This photograph captured the joy and relief felt by everyone on the team. What I love so much about the snapshot is that the excitement wasn't really about the specific person who had made the play—everyone on the team and everyone in the stands celebrated because of what it meant for the entire team.

While most sports teams naturally function in this way, having a similar "team" mindset is much harder in day-to-day life. When someone succeeds or accomplishes something we wish we could do, it is difficult not to be envious of them, isn't it? We may celebrate them to their face, but in our hearts, we are often jealous. God knew we would struggle with envy. In fact, he added it to the Ten Commandments. He said, "You shall not covet your neighbor's house. You shall not covet your neighbor's wife, or his male or female servant, his ox or donkey, or anything that belongs to your neighbor" (Exodus 20:17). Basically, God is saying we shouldn't resent others who have what we lack. To stop or prevent envious behavior, we need to practice being content with what God has given to us and celebrate what God has given to others.

In the book of Luke, we witness this attitude of contentment and celebration in the life of Elizabeth. She was childless at an old age, and in societies like Israel, a woman's value was largely measured by her ability to bear children. I imagine that Elizabeth spent much of her life navigating feelings of envy as other women become mothers. But in God's time, she became pregnant with John the Baptist. Elizabeth's cousin Mary also unexpectedly became pregnant with Jesus around the same time.

After the angel of the Lord appeared to Elizabeth and Mary separately, Mary went to visit her relative. Elizabeth met Mary with excitement for what the Lord was doing in her life. She could have been jealous that Mary's son would be greater than her own, but she celebrated the goodness and faithfulness of God to them both. They were instantly bound together by these miracles of God. Because of Elizabeth's joyous reaction, Mary sang with praise her song "The Magnificat," and she stayed with Elizabeth for three more months. Elizabeth's reaction had a meaningful impact on Mary's attitude toward her assignment (Luke 1:46–56).

Our reaction to and celebration of our friends and family can have the same significant effect. What is your response when someone succeeds or is honored? What about when God gives someone a special blessing? A cure for jealousy is to celebrate with those individuals, realizing that God uses his people in ways best suited to his purpose. Scripture tells us to "rejoice with those who rejoice" (Romans 12:15). Therefore, if a person is blessed or succeeds in God's work, rejoice in it because we are all on God's team with the same end goal in mind. And spoiler alert, we are on the winning team!

Your Little Task

When you hear someone sharing good news, do you react with jealousy or celebration? Be intentional about celebrating others even for small victories. Watch how they react as you cheer them on.

Prayer Prompt

Lord, thank you for how you've created me and for the unique blessings and gifts you have given me. When I start feeling envious of another person, remind me to celebrate with them. Help me to realize we are on the same team and that anything from you is worth celebrating. Amen.

A Little Time

*What is your life? You are a mist
that appears for a little while and then vanishes.*

JAMES 4:14

I dropped my son, Will, off at school one morning, and because of extracurricular activities, he was gone until late in the evening. By the time he returned home, it had been thirteen hours since I'd seen him. Every day is not this way, but he's growing up, and more and more, this routine is becoming our new norm.

Not so long ago, he was always with me. First in my womb and then in my arms. As he grew, that shifted to my lap, and when he was too big for that, we still held hands. We ate meals together, played together, ran errands together, and when I was really tired, we napped together.

I admit that on many days in those early years of motherhood I longed for a break from the constant togetherness. I craved time for myself without a little one always needing something from me.

Now, I long to have that kind of togetherness back again. Thankfully, even though our relationship is changing, on most days he walks through the door, greets me with a hug, and sits down to talk. Despite the recent scarcity of our time together, our love has remained close. For that, I'm so grateful.

In my heart of hearts, I know my son will never stop needing me. Maybe not as much as he once did, but I have a lot of mothering yet to do and so much love still to give.

And so, while we are together, I make the most of the time we do have and commit to being more intentional. The car rides, ball games, homework, movie nights, church services, and family trips are more sacred now—especially now that I realize how quickly this motherhood journey is passing by.

How ironic that all those days I wished away are the same ones I'm wishing to have back. I pray I remember this lesson in this current season and the seasons to come. Before long, Will is going to be out of the house altogether, and I'll see him even less. But I trust there will be beauty in that season as well, as there has been in every one to date. There is a time for everything and a season for every activity under heaven (Ecclesiastes 3:1), and whatever season it is, I want to steward my time well as a mother, wife, daughter, and friend. I have no doubt the same is true of you.

The apostle James says, "What is your life? You are a mist that appears for a little while and then vanishes" (James 4:14). Psalm 90 shares something similar when the psalmist reminds us that a thousand years are like a day to the Lord. Realizing our days are numbered helps us to steward the little time we have wisely and for eternal good. If we have something important we want to do, we must not put it off for a better day. Because life is short, we shouldn't neglect what is truly important. Time is but a vapor, and we can't get it back.

Your Little Task

Ask God to reveal the value of the moments in your life. Make space to intentionally focus on these moments and cherish each one.

Lord, help me to be intentional with the time you have given me. Forgive me for wishing my days away. Show me where I am wasting my time and where I need to devote it. Lead me to spend my time in ways that have eternal value. Amen.

A Little Touch

A man with leprosy came and knelt in front of Jesus, begging to be healed. "If you are willing, you can heal me and make me clean," he said. Moved with compassion, Jesus reached out and touched him. "I am willing," he said. "Be healed!"

MARK 1:40–41 NLT

When my husband, Bryan, comes home from work each day, my daughter, Kate, runs to him and jumps into his arms to give him a hug. More often than not, Bryan says, "I needed that," as he holds her tight.

There is just something comforting about the touch of a loved one, isn't there? An encouraging pat on the back, a reassuring squeeze of the hand, a playful rustle of the hair, a quick kiss on the forehead, or a lingering embrace—these kinds of touches can strengthen our connection, soothe our emotions, and communicate understanding without a word. From the moment we are born to the final days of our lives, touch is an integral part of the human experience, impacting our physical, mental, and emotional health.

Jesus understood the power of touch. He held children, washed feet, and healed the sick through physical touch. In one of the first recorded healings Jesus performed, he healed a leper by touching him. Everyone considered lepers to be untouchable—everyone but Jesus (Mark 1). I love this about him, but interestingly, this wasn't always how Jesus healed lepers. In fact, in Luke 17, when Jesus met ten lepers in a village, he didn't touch them.

Instead, he told them to go see the priest, and while they were on their way there, they were cleansed (Luke 17:12–14).

So in one instance, Jesus touched a leper to heal him, and in another instance, he didn't touch the ten lepers to heal them. This has me wondering why. Clearly, Jesus could heal without touching someone, so why touch this man when he didn't have to? We find the answer in Mark 1:41, which says, "Moved with compassion, Jesus reached out and touched him" (NLT). There was something this man needed that others didn't; he needed to be touched.

This leper example in Mark isn't the only time Jesus touched people to heal them. Through touch, he healed the fever of Peter's mother-in-law (Mark 1:29–31), raised a young girl from the dead (Mark 5:41), returned hearing to the deaf (Mark 7:33–36), and restored sight to the blind (Mark 8:22–25).

On another occasion, as Jesus was walking, a woman who had been bleeding for twelve years touched the hem of his cloak (Mark 5:25–34). Just touching him was all it took to heal her. It's fascinating to note that in these passages it doesn't make a difference if Jesus was the one who reached out to the person or if it was the person who reached out to Jesus. As long as contact was made in faith, there was healing power in the touch.

Nearly nineteen centuries later, these stories are still affecting our hearts. One touch from Jesus has now affected millions, and he wants to do the same thing in our lives. Just as Jesus was moved by compassion, compassion can move us to reach out to others too. Your simple, wordless gestures could be exactly what is needed to strengthen a connection, soothe an emotion, communicate without a word, or heal a hurting heart. Does someone need a touch from you today?

Your Little Task

Offer a handshake, pat on the back, hug, or a hand to hold. Don't be surprised if the person you reach out to responds with, "I needed that!"

Prayer Prompt

Lord, thank you for the sense of touch. Help me to use my physical contact to display your love and care for others. May my gestures be healing rather than hurtful. Touch my heart so I can touch the hearts of others for you. Amen.

A Little Prayer

In the same way, the Spirit helps us in our weakness. We do not know what we ought to pray for, but the Spirit himself intercedes for us through wordless groans. And he who searches our hearts knows the mind of the Spirit because the Spirit intercedes for God's people in accordance with the will of God.

ROMANS 8:26–27

A friend sent me a text asking for prayer. "Of course," I quickly responded, feeling honored she thought to ask me. But several days later, when she texted about something else, I realized I'd never prayed.

Not an honorable moment after all.

Unfortunately, this wasn't the first time I'd enthusiastically agreed to pray for a friend or an acquaintance and failed to follow through. I'm not sure if these lapses in prayer happened because I forgot, because I was busy, or because I thought my prayers wouldn't make a difference.

Regardless of the reasons why I sometimes fail to pray, I desire to be a woman of my word. After all, I want the people in my life to follow through when I request prayer. Despite any second-guessing, I do believe in the power of prayer. As unfathomable as it may seem, God allows our prayers to impact the world. We see the significance of prayers offered on behalf of others over and over again in the Bible.

For the sake of his nephew Lot, Abraham prayed for the people of Sodom, and Lot's family was saved from destruction (Genesis 18:23–33).

When the people of Israel were sinning and God was planning their destruction, Moses prayed for God's mercy, and the Lord relented (Exodus 32:9–14; Numbers 14:11–20).

Daniel prayed for his people in Judah. Not only were Daniel and his friends saved, but they were also elevated to positions of high authority (Daniel 9:3–19).

Hezekiah prayed when the Assyrian king laid siege to Jerusalem, and God waged a war on their behalf (2 Kings 19:19).

The church prayed for Peter when he was in prison, and God sent an angel to rescue him (Acts 12:1–17).

Paul prayed regularly for the people he served, and we are still reaping the benefits of his heartfelt prayers (Romans 1:9–10; 10:1; Ephesians 1:15–19; Philippians 1:3–11; 1 Thessalonians 3:9–13).

And, of course, Jesus modeled the importance of praying for others when he interceded for his disciples, for children, and for us as future believers (John 17). In fact, Jesus is still interceding for us at the right hand of God, advocating on our behalf (Romans 8:34).

If we know God's power is infinitely greater than ours, it only makes sense to rely on it, right? So, whether in public or in private, with many words or with few, with eyes closed or with eyes wide open, at morning or at night, we simply must talk to God and leave the results up to him.

Even in those situations when we don't have the words to pray, we can trust the Holy Spirit to intercede for us. And friend, he never fails to follow through.

Your Little Task

Think of someone in your life who needs prayer. Bow your head and pray.

Lord, forgive me for not following through and praying for those in my life. Help me intentionally and mindfully bring their requests to you, align my requests with your will, and increase my belief that you not only hear our requests, but you also respond to them. Amen.

A Little Faith

Without faith it is impossible to please God.
HEBREWS 11:6

One morning at the gym, I was lifting weights and was surprised by how light they felt. I had recently established a new routine of dropping the kids off at school and working out right after. I hadn't been training long, but already I noticed I was getting stronger, and I realized I needed to add more weight if I wanted to continue challenging my muscles. At that moment, I thought about how our faith is like a muscle. It grows with exercise, gaining strength over time. Only instead of growing through the lifting of physical weights, our faith grows through trusting and obeying God, which is demonstrated by intentional action.

Hebrews 11 is often called the Faith Hall of Fame because it celebrates the lives of those who were commended for their faith. Once, as I read through this chapter, I underlined every action word that was associated with a person's faith. By faith Abel offered, Enoch was taken, Noah built, Abraham obeyed and went, Isaac and Jacob blessed, Moses persevered, and Joshua marched. Others conquered, administered, shut, quenched, escaped, welcomed, and faced. They were commended for their faith in action. Yes, we are saved by faith alone, but I'm convinced that if we settle for mere acknowledgment of God's existence, we are living an incomplete faith. Our faith grows and is made complete by what we do.

Even though I want a complete faith, it's easier said than done (pun intended). If you're anything like me, I feel a bit overwhelmed by the Hebrews 11 list of faith in action. I can't shut the mouth of a lion or quench the fury of flames! Thankfully, even though faith is made complete by our actions, ultimately, it isn't about us—it is about God. We can be certain God is who he says he is and will do what he says he will do. God is powerful enough to do the things we can't, and we have his Spirit working in and through us.

In fact, something else I noticed in Hebrews 11 is that those listed in the faith's hall of fame are people whose weaknesses turned to strength. Now that sounds like something I can surely relate to! Since we have the Holy Spirit dwelling inside of us, we can act in faith no matter how weak we feel. We can offer all we are to him in faith and believe that it's enough. It may be as simple as by faith we cooked, cleaned, taught, moved, wrote, hosted, walked, or prayed.

The key is to be faithful in the doing. Just as our spiritual forefathers didn't always experience what was promised this side of heaven, we may not either. Even if we don't see the result of our faith in action, we can trust he has something better planned when we are all together one day (Hebrews 11:40). On that day I pray we, too, are commended for our faith. What will you do by faith today?

Your Little Task

Read Hebrews 11 and think about what the heroes of faith were commended for. Finish this sentence: By faith (your name)…

Lord, may I not be of little faith, but instead, may I one day be commended for great faith. I know this kind of faith isn't about me, rather it is about you and what you can do. Help me to grasp the truth that I am saved by faith alone but that my deeds prove my faith is genuine. Turn my weaknesses to strengths as I act in faith today. Amen.

A Little Conversation

The tongue has the power of life and death.
PROVERBS 18:21

I once read an article about a man in San Francisco who was going to commit suicide by jumping off the Golden Gate Bridge. He left a note in his apartment saying that he would not jump if on the way to the bridge one person smiled and said hello to him. The man jumped. He miraculously survived, but he was severely injured. Isn't it shocking that not one person in such a populated city smiled or said hello? What if they had? A simple greeting could have prevented injury and saved a life.[1]

I'm convicted as I retell this story because I wonder if I would have said hello. How many people do I pass every single day yet never acknowledge? I don't know about you, but I'm even guilty of purposefully avoiding talking to others. I put in earbuds on a walk or at the gym, which signals to everyone around me that I'm uninterested in conversation. I stick my nose in a book when I'm on the airplane and keep my eyes fixed on my phone when I'm sitting on the bleachers and the game isn't in progress. Sometimes when I see a person I know at a store, I dart into another aisle to avoid them, especially if I still have on yesterday's makeup. I regretfully admit I've even silenced a phone call or ignored a text because I was not ready to converse at that moment. Honestly,

---

[1] Tad Friend, "Jumpers: The Fatal Grandeur of the Golden Gate Bridge," *New Yorker*, October 5, 2003, https://www.newyorker.com/magazine/2003/10/13/jumpers.

I have used my introverted nature as an excuse for far too long. How can we lead someone to Jesus if we don't even start the conversation?

Who better to look to than Jesus for guidance on how to dialogue with people. The four Gospels record more than forty meetings between him and various individuals. In nine of these cases, it was Jesus who initiated the conversations. In twenty-five instances, it was the other party who started the discussion, and the remaining six were triggered by third parties. But on every occasion, Jesus chose to engage and keep the conversation going.

These conversations took place in various locations, but the majority of the interactions occurred in the workplace and in homes. Interestingly enough, very few took place in religious settings. Instead, Jesus discussed topics of eternal significance wherever he happened to be when he met others.

Jesus' conversations went way beyond meaningless chit-chat and brief pleasantries. In more than half of the recorded conversations in Scripture, he asked questions. Even though he knew how others would respond, he showed his desire to continue the conversation and create connection and fellowship.

Do you have a desire for connection and fellowship with others? As I think about my most cherished relationships, almost all of them started with a hello. Like Jesus, we should be prepared to take initiative as well as respond to the initiative of others, no matter the time or location. Though it is small and simple, there is immense power in our tongue. I pray we use our words for the glory of God and for the blessing of others. Because what starts as small talk can turn into an encounter that saves someone from untimely physical death or even helps them find eternal salvation. One little word can make all the difference.

Say hello to the next person you pass. If someone speaks to you, engage with them and continue the conversation.

Prayer Prompt

Lord, thank you for wanting to connect and have fellowship with me. Help me to follow your example of initiating and engaging in conversation. Stir in my heart a desire for a relationship with others. Give me the courage to step out of my comfort zone and be vulnerable with the people you put in my path. May the words that come from my mouth edify others and glorify you. Let me be your mouthpiece. Amen.

A Little Money

"Truly I tell you, this poor widow has put more into the treasury than all the others. They all gave out of their wealth; but she, out of her poverty, put in everything—all she had to live on."

MARK 12:43–44; CF. LUKE 21:1–4

"Close your eyes. I have a surprise for you," my daughter, Kate, instructed, grabbing my hand to guide me. "You can open your eyes now," she proudly exclaimed as she thrust open the door to her room.

I stood at the doorway, scanning the room in awe. Plush pillows and blankets were thoughtfully placed upon the floor in a makeshift seating arrangement for two. Christmas lights lined the area, flickering to generate an enchanting glow. The smells of buttery popcorn filled the air, open cans of soda fizzed, and music from a movie trailer floated from the TV. A poster board sign written in marker read, "Mom and Kate night," explaining the entire evening set up.

"It's perfect," I remarked as we snuggled into the cozy spot she had created with things gathered from around our home.

Several weeks later, I decided to reciprocate her thoughtful gesture. I headed to the local dollar store to get my creative juices flowing. Ten dollars later, I had purchased items for a spa-themed girls' night. When Kate came home from school and saw her surprise, she squealed with delight! We dressed in our fuzzy robes and slippers, lit candles, turned on soothing music, painted our nails, drank chamomile tea from antique china teacups, massaged each other's shoulders, and applied face masks topped off with cucumber slices on our eyes.

"This is one of the best nights ever," Kate declared afterward. And I wholeheartedly agreed.

That evening, as I reflected on our time together, I was struck by how a little money went a long way to create a beautiful memory for us. While big vacations and expensive purchases can be nice, so can things from the dollar store. When we use a little creativity and give gifts from our hearts, even items that are free can have a big impact.

Activities like baking a cake, coloring a picture, completing a puzzle, playing a board game, watching the sunset, packing a picnic, swimming in a lake, walking in the park, or building a crackling campfire don't cost much, but the return on investment is great—a large deposit in our hearts.

This principle is beautifully displayed in the life of a poor widow who gave all she had in the Gospels of Mark and Luke. This small portion of Scripture is recorded in only three verses, however, the lesson it holds is priceless.

The story of the widow's mite begins with Jesus sitting with his disciples near the temple treasury, watching people give their monetary offerings. The rich contributed large sums of money while the widow gave only two copper coins. These mites were the smallest coin denomination. Together they equaled only a penny.

While her donation was meager in comparison to those of the other givers that day, Jesus drew the disciples' attention to her offering in particular. He said, "Truly I tell you, this poor widow has put more into the treasury than all the others. They all gave out of their wealth; but she, out of her poverty, put in everything— all she had to live on" (Mark 12:43–44; cf. Luke 21:1–4).

I love that Jesus valued her humble gift. His comment verifies that no amount of money is too small. From our earthly perspective, we question how in the world her minuscule donation could make any difference, but to Jesus, it made all the difference in the world.

Clearly, her act moved Jesus enough to record it in the Bible for future generations. Because she gave all she had, it didn't matter that the offering was small. It was big in proportion to the others—it was bigger in heart. Her paltry donation proved that she was purely devoted to him. Jesus used the little money she had to teach a lesson about the heart of giving and show that any amount spent from the heart can yield an eternal dividend.

Your Little Task

Spend money on someone else today. Let the Lord lead you on whom to bless.

Prayer Prompt

Lord, I know any money I have is yours. Every good and perfect gift comes from you, and that includes money. Reinforce in my mind that I am a steward and not an owner of the resources I have been given. Help me make investments in people. Give me your generous heart so I can be a cheerful giver to others. Settle in my soul that it is not the amount I give but the heart in which I give it. Amen.

DAY 25

A Little Effort

Some men came, bringing to him a paralyzed man, carried by four
of them. Since they could not get him to Jesus because of the crowd,
they made an opening in the roof above Jesus by digging through it
and then lowered the mat the man was lying on.

MARK 2:3–4

My dad very rarely misses my kids' extracurricular activities. He
makes an effort to attend as many of their events as his schedule
will allow, regardless of the weather or the location of the activity.
Whether they are on the sidelines, court, bleachers, pool deck, or
auditorium stage, my kids can look up to see his smiling face there
to support them. He did the same thing for my brothers and me
when we were growing up. We knew we were a priority to him,
and his effort to show up was proof. He doesn't have to be there,
but he wants to be, and it makes my children and me feel loved.

It means so much when people make an effort for us,
doesn't it? God appreciates our effort too. As unfathomable as
it seems, God chooses to use us to fulfill his purposes on earth.
He could easily do it all on his own, and there is no doubt he is
in control, but he often requires our participation before he acts.
Throughout Scripture, we see that he works through those willing
to make an effort for him.

Of course, our levels of effort can vary, but one of my
favorite examples of a display of extra effort is from Mark 2.
It all started when people heard that Jesus had come home to
Capernaum. They gathered in such large numbers that there was

no room left in the house where Jesus was, not even outside the door. As Jesus preached the Word to the people, four men came, carrying a paralyzed man. Since they could not get him to Jesus because of the crowd, they made an opening in the roof above Jesus by digging through it and then lowered the mat the man was lying on. When Jesus saw their faith, he forgave the paralyzed man of his sins. He then told the man to "get up, take your mat and go home." So the man got up, took his mat, and walked out in full view of them all. This amazed everyone, and they all praised God (Mark 2:1–12).

After reading this account and putting myself into the place of these four friends, I wonder if it would have occurred to me to help my paralyzed friend in the first place. I'd like to think I would have, but the more likely scenario is that I would have been more concerned about hearing Jesus or getting healing for myself.

Even if I had the intention of helping my friend, seeing such a large crowd would have caused me to hesitate. When I realized the door was blocked, I'm not so sure I would have pursued an alternative and likely would have given up, shrugging my shoulders and feeling proud of myself for trying at all. But these men didn't stop at the crowd or at the door; instead, they plotted and planned an alternative route. And this route involved a lot of effort.

Houses in Bible times were built of stone and had flat roofs made of mud mixed with straw. These men carried their friend up the outside stairway to the roof. It took four of them (v. 3), so he must have been heavy. Once they were on top of the house, they took apart as much of the mud and straw mixture as was necessary to lower their paralyzed friend in front of Jesus. Digging a hole and lowering him down took a lot of work! They allowed no obstacle to prevent them from helping their friend.

In this story, I also notice the effort of the paralyzed man. If you'll remember, Jesus healed the man's spiritual life first, forgiving his sins because of his friends' faith. But then, in order for his physical body to be healed, Jesus required effort from him. The paralyzed man had to get up, take his mat, and go home. The man obeyed, and as a result, he received his healing, but not until he took action.

I'm convicted as I read this short story of faith, action, and effort. On a personal level, it causes me to ponder if God is waiting for me to show effort and take action before healing me physically and spiritually. Is he waiting for you? On a communal level, am I moved to action when I see a need? These are challenging thoughts. There are so many people who have physical and spiritual needs we can meet. Human need moved these four men. I pray we allow human need to compel us to compassionate action as well. Let's make an effort and allow nothing to stop us from bringing others to the feet of Jesus.

Your Little Task

Ask God to open your spiritual eyes to see the needs of others. Be intentional to prioritize meeting those needs.

Prayer Prompt

Lord, thank you for meeting all of my needs. I come to your feet for healing. Forgive me for not being concerned about the needs of others, being lackadaisical, and giving up too soon. Strengthen me and embolden me to care for others enough to bring them to you. Amen.

A Little Humility

Pride goes before destruction,
a haughty spirit before a fall.
PROVERBS 16:18

Around the dinner table one evening, my family and I were discussing the phrase "built different." I'm unsure of the phrase's origin, but it refers to a person who is uniquely better than others in some way, and it is often used to describe a person's performance in a given situation.

During the conversation, my husband, Bryan, pointed out that, as Christians, instead of focusing on being built different, we should adjust our mindset to remember that God is *building different*. The term *built* suggests we are finished growing and have reached the pinnacle. *Building*, on the other hand, suggests the process is not complete and that there is still work to be done. This mindset shift creates a humble posture in our hearts as we recall we aren't better than anyone else. We know it is God who is great, not us, and he is the one who helps us grow and develop.

In Christian terms, this process of development is called *sanctification*. *To sanctify* literally means "to set apart for special use or purpose," that is, to make holy or sacred. This process is not complete until we reach heaven.

As I think about these two mindsets, I see that one has a prideful posture of human glorification, while the other is a humble demeanor of God glorification. In our own lives, this looks like pointing to God, who rightfully deserves the credit, rather than pointing to ourselves in every success or accomplishment. When we credit ourselves, we are being prideful, and pride tops the list of sins that God hates (Proverbs 6:16–17). The opposite of this detestable attitude is humility.

John the Baptist epitomized a humble spirit. To put his story into context, we need to remember that Israel had not seen a prophet for more than four hundred years. People were eagerly awaiting the Messiah, so when John began prophesying, many confused him for the long-awaited Savior.

John was definitely different. He wore odd clothes, ate strange food, and preached an unusual message. He was a loner who lived in the desert and had no power or position in the Jewish political system.

God had certainly set John apart. He spoke with almost irresistible authority, and as a result, numerous people responded to his message of repentance. However, even as people crowded to him, he pointed beyond himself, never forgetting that his main role was to announce the arrival of Jesus.

Although John was so well-known, he was content for Jesus to take the higher place. When the people questioned who he was, John responded that he was not even worthy to be Christ's slave, to perform the humble task of unfastening his shoes (John 1:27). Interestingly enough, Jesus said John was the greatest of all the prophets (Luke 7:28). If such a great person felt inadequate even to be Christ's slave, how much more should we lay aside our pride?

When we truly understand who Christ is, our self-importance melts away. This is true humility, the basis for greatness in any work we do for the Lord. May we have the humble posture of John the Baptist so that we can allow God to build a different kind of kingdom through us.

Your Little Task

Reflect on the gifts God has given you. Give him all the glory for any success or accomplishment in your life.

Prayer Prompt

Lord, reinforce in my heart that my purpose is to point people to you. Forgive me for the times I have acted pridefully. I know you oppose the proud and show favor to the humble. Help me be content to let you take the higher place. Amen.

A Little Hospitality

As Jesus and his disciples were on their way, he came to a village where a woman named Martha opened her home to him. She had a sister called Mary, who sat at the Lord's feet listening to what he said.

LUKE 10:38–39

"Would you like a reader for your manuscript before you turn it in to your publisher?" a fellow swim team mom generously offered.

"Sure!" I responded immediately because, little did she know, I'd been praying for another set of eyes to give me feedback.

Megan's family had just moved to our community, and this conversation occurred the first time we met. We exchanged numbers and more pleasantries then gathered our kids to leave. When I returned home, Megan sent me a text reiterating her offer. I mustered up the courage to send her my heart on the page, honestly not expecting much in response.

The next day, Megan sent me a picture of my manuscript—she had printed it, hole-punched it, and placed it neatly in a binder to read. We agreed to meet the next week so I could hear her thoughts. I was thinking we'd meet at a local coffee shop for an hour or so, but instead, she invited me to her home.

When I arrived at her house the following week, she opened the door and welcomed me with a warm smile. Once inside, she ushered me into a tidy kitchen. The smell of flavored coffee wafted through the air, and a lemon poppyseed Bundt cake sat atop a glass cake stand on the counter. As I scanned the kitchen, tears glistened in my eyes. "You did all this for me?" I asked, baffled by the extent of her effort.

We worked for hours, combing through the manuscript, which she had thoughtfully marked with her sharpened pencil. We refilled our coffee cups and brainstormed through lunch. Megan must have heard my stomach grumbling because she got up from the table and headed to the refrigerator. She began cutting cheeses and deli meats and neatly placed them on a platter, along with crackers and an assortment of vegetables for us to snack on. Before I knew it, it was almost 3:00 p.m., and I needed to pick up my kids from school. "Let's do this again next week," she offered as I left. Again, I teared up, overwhelmed by her loving care.

As I drove away and reflected on my time with Megan, I was in awe of her hospitality. Not only did she care for me physically, but she also cared for me spiritually and emotionally. It inspired me to make others who come to my home feel the way she made me feel.

When we think of hospitality in the Bible, typically the story of Mary and Martha comes to mind (Luke 10). Jesus was their frequent guest, and for Mary, hospitality meant giving more attention to her guest's words than to the cleanliness of her home or the timeliness of her meals. She let her older sister, Martha, take care of those details. This bothered Martha, so she brought her concern to Jesus. But Jesus said, "Martha, Martha…you are worried and upset about many things, but few things are needed—or indeed only one. Mary has chosen what is better, and it will not be taken away from her" (Luke 10:41–42).

When we hear this story, we usually think we need to be more like Mary, since Martha's priorities were the ones Jesus corrected. But, as I think about my friend Megan, it occurs to me that she was both a Martha and a Mary. While hospitality can happen in a messy home with no food on the table, it's also not wrong to thoughtfully clean, cook, and prepare for a guest. The key is to also focus on spending time with the person in order to make them feel comfortable and at home, just as Megan did for me.

Romans 12:13 tells us to "practice hospitality." Many people believe hospitality is a gift we either have or don't. However, this Scripture communicates that hospitality should be offered repeatedly regardless of how skilled we are. It is important to God and worth pursuing. Maybe it's time to put out a welcome mat.

Your Little Task

Whom do you feel God is leading you to host in your home? How can you prepare and be present with that person?

Prayer Prompt

Father, thank you for preparing a room for me and inviting me into your forever home. Help me to be hospitable and welcoming to the people you place in my life. Free me from the pressure to make myself look good, and instead, lead me to care for the needs of others so they feel good. Amen.

A Little Grace

*"Let any one of you who is without sin
be the first to throw a stone at her."*
JOHN 8:7

The first time I saw my husband, he had a black eye. My immediate thought was, *He sure is cute, but I'll bet he's trouble. I'd better stay away from him.* I imagine God getting a good chuckle from this first interaction. He knew what Bryan would mean to me in the future, but I didn't.

Later, I learned the real reason behind his questionable appearance. He was a college athlete, and the black eye was from playing competitively during practice earlier that day. We laugh about it now, but I can't help thinking: *What if I had let my inaccurate judgment prevent him from becoming my husband? What a tragedy that would have been to my now-happy family of four.*

In the Gospel of John, Jesus addressed judgmental attitudes when the teachers of the law and the Pharisees brought a woman caught in adultery into the temple. "They made her stand before the group and said to Jesus, 'Teacher, this woman was caught in the act of adultery. In the Law Moses commanded us to stone such women. Now, what do you say?'" (8:2–6).

Rather than judging her, "Jesus bent down and started to write on the ground with his finger. When [the religious leaders] kept on questioning him, he straightened up and said to them, 'Let any one of you who is without sin be the first to throw a stone at her.' Again, he stooped down and wrote on the ground" (8:6–8).

Starting with the older ones, those gathered around started to leave, until only Jesus and the woman were left. "Jesus straightened up and asked her, 'Woman, where are they? Has no one condemned you?'

"'No one, sir,' she said.

"'Then neither do I condemn you,' Jesus declared. 'Go now and leave your life of sin'" (8:9–11).

This act was a bold statement about judging others. Because Jesus upheld the legal penalty for adultery, which was stoning, he could not be accused of going against the law. By saying that only a sinless person could throw the first stone, he highlighted the importance of grace. He wasn't condoning the woman's behavior, but he was compassionate toward her.

While we may not literally be stoning people, we do pass judgment when others are caught in sin. However, in doing so, we act as though we have never sinned. I think that's why Jesus told us in Matthew, "Do not judge, or you too will be judged. For in the same way you judge others, you will be judged, and with the measure you use, it will be measured to you. Why do you look at the speck of sawdust in your brother's eye and pay no attention to the plank in your own eye?" (7:1–3).

Thinking back to when I saw Bryan's literal black eye for the first time and how I assumed that he was trouble convicts me. How many relationships have I missed out on because I was casting stones? How many people could I have pointed to God if I had responded with grace rather than judgment? I pray we put down our stones and pick up the practices of our Savior instead. It is God's role to judge, not ours. Our role is to extend grace whether we think the other person deserves it or not. We can give grace freely because it is freely given to us.

Your Little Task

Thank God for his undeserved favor. Ask him to reveal whether you have been judgmental and whether there is someone in your life to whom you need to extend grace. Settle that in your heart today and, if you need to, tell the other person.

Prayer Prompt

Lord, I know your grace is sufficient for me, and it is undeserved. Forgive me for the times I've been too quick to judge others. You alone can judge. Replace any judgment with your grace. Amen.

Day 29

A Little Inclusion

Know that the LORD is God.
It is he who made us, and we are his;
we are his people, the sheep of his pasture.

PSALM 100:3

I once saw a picture online of many of my friends celebrating a birthday. The caption read, "So much fun getting together with all of my friends." *I guess they don't consider me their friend*, I thought, deeply hurt by the exclusion.

We all have an innate desire to belong. When we are excluded, whether someone does it intentionally or unintentionally, it doesn't matter—both are painful. It comforts me to remember that Jesus himself felt excluded. Scripture tells us, "[Jesus] was in the world, and though the world was made through him, the world did not recognize him. He came to that which was his own, but his own did not receive him" (John 1:10–11).

Doesn't it amaze you that, although Jesus created the world, the people he created didn't recognize him? However, the good news for us is there is a "yet" in the verses that follow this sad reality. They read, "Yet to all those who received him, to those who believed in his name, he gave the right to become children of God—children born not of natural descent, nor of human decision or of a husband's will, but born of God" (John 1:12–13).

In essence, God is saying that being born of God places you in his family. This truth alone reassures us that regardless of where or whether we belong in an earthly sense, we forever belong to him.

Knowing his secure place in the family of God, Jesus intentionally and lovingly pursued those who felt excluded. One person he pursued was Zacchaeus. He was a chief tax collector, and tax collectors were among the most unpopular people in Israel. When Jesus was teaching, Zacchaeus had a hard time seeing him, in part because he was short. It's also likely that, due to their dislike of him, the other Jews prevented Zacchaeus from getting close to Jesus. So, in an effort to get a better view, Zacchaeus climbed a tree. When Jesus reached the tree, he looked up and invited himself to Zacchaeus' home. All the people saw this and began to mutter in disapproval that Jesus was going to be the guest of a sinner, but Jesus joined him anyway. Through this interaction, Zacchaeus repented, and his life was radically transformed. He found belonging with Jesus (Luke 19).

Maybe, like me, you've had experiences that have made you feel excluded. But as we see in Scripture, the biggest crowds and groups aren't always right. Look at the Pharisees and the crowds that crucified Jesus. As painful as it seems, sometimes it is in our best interest not to fit into the "popular" earthly groups. We find our belonging in Jesus, knowing we are a part of his family. God sent his Son Jesus for all the world, and Jesus died for all of our sins (John 3:16). Everyone is included, and that includes you. With this knowledge, I pray we follow Jesus' lead to pursue, invite, and love others who may be feeling excluded. They need to know they can find belonging with him too.

Your Little Task

Think about whether you have a tendency to exclude others. Then, the next time you are in a social environment, take notice of your surroundings and look for ways to include someone who may feel left out.

Prayer Prompt

God, thank you for giving your one and only Son for the world. Jesus, thank you for dying on the cross for all of our sins. I take comfort in knowing I always belong with you. Remind me of the ways you include and love every single person, especially those who are typically excluded. Soften my heart to notice, pursue, invite, and love those who might be feeling left out so they may find belonging in you too. Amen.

A Little Testimony

*"They triumphed over him by the blood of the Lamb
and by the word of their testimony."*
REVELATION 12:11

For the longest time, I doubted the power of my testimony because, when I became a Christian, there was no dramatic change in my attitude or behavior, no drastic before and after. Rather, the change I've experienced has happened gradually. Slowly, I have learned of God's love and grace. First, he was only my Savior. I was saved out of fear, out of a simple desire to not go to hell. Then, when I became a parent, I learned to see him as my Father and myself as his beloved daughter. As time passed, I eventually surrendered to him as my Lord, praying that my desires would align with his. Now, I'm starting to recognize him as my favorite person to talk to and be with. I'm beginning to know him as my friend. This is my testimony—my story God continues to write.

What is your testimony? Have you ever had a hard time articulating it or believing in its power? While our experiences with Jesus may vary greatly, the impact of sharing them does not. In fact, Scripture tells us the devil is defeated by the blood of the Lamb and by the word of our testimony (Revelation 12:11). Jesus already completed his part, and now, it's our turn to follow through with ours.

Consider for a moment how your life might have unfolded if someone hadn't shared their testimony with you. Because those who have gone before us were faithful to their mission, we heard the good news and had the opportunity to believe. Now we have the same responsibility to tell others about his saving grace. Once we experience him, we are meant to become witnesses for him. Their eternal salvation is at stake. This is the Great Commission—to "go and make disciples of all nations" (Matthew 28:19).

In Matthew 28, we find a beautiful example of two women doing just this. After Jesus' death on the cross, Mary Magdalene and the other Mary went to the tomb with spices and perfumes. When they arrived, an angel said, "He is not here; he has risen, just as he said. Come and see the place where he lay. Then go quickly and tell his disciples: 'He has risen from the dead'" (Matthew 28:6–7). The women left the tomb with great joy and ran to report it to the disciples. The same instruction is given to us: Come and see, then go and tell.

After this tomb experience, one of the disciples, Peter, wrote that we should always be ready to give an answer when asked about our faith (1 Peter 3:15). He learned this lesson the hard way after he had denied knowing Christ three times before his crucifixion (Luke 22:54–62). May we learn from his hard-fought wisdom to always be prepared to give an answer to everyone who asks us to give the reason for the hope that we have.

Are you prepared to tell others what Christ has done for you? We don't hesitate to tell others about makeup products, cleaning hacks, favorite recipes, money-saving deals, books we've read, and movies we've watched. So why do we hesitate to tell others about Jesus? We share what we love, and what could transform someone's life more than a relationship with him?

We don't have to have any special skill to be a witness for Christ. Simply tell your God story and how he has changed your life. This is how the gospel is spread. Your testimony could be the reason someone else can have a testimony of their own.

Your Little Task

Reflect on your testimony to see how God has been present in your life.

Prayer Prompt

Father, thank you for loving me so personally. I am grateful for your work for me and within me. Help me to realize the power of my testimony and give me the willingness to share it with others. Open up opportunities for me to witness for you. Give me the words to say and the courage to share your good news. Amen.

A Little Tradition

"This is a day you are to commemorate; for the generations to come you shall celebrate it as a festival to the LORD—a lasting ordinance."

We called her "Munder" because when my brothers and I were first learning to talk we couldn't pronounce all the syllables in *grandmother*. She lived several hours away, and I always looked forward to visiting her, especially during the holidays. More than anything else, I remember how spending time with her made me feel loved and cared for. I was her only granddaughter, and so I think that brought about an extra special connection between us.

One of the things I remember most were the meals and treats Munder made. She grew raspberries along her fence, and my brothers and I would help her pick them. With these raspberries, Munder made jelly, which she spread on thin French pancakes called *crepes*. She rolled the crepes into a flute shape and sprinkled them with powdered sugar. To this day, every time I eat a rasp-berry or a crepe, I think of her.

Munder has since gone on to be with the Lord. It's amazing how little things make me remember her, especially the holiday traditions she passed on to us that she learned from her own mother. Since she passed, my family has tried to include many of Munder's recipes on our menu. I'm grateful that I have her hand-written recipe cards so I can replicate her specialties for my family. It makes me feel like I'm still with her in the kitchen. No holiday is complete unless nutmeg logs, snickerdoodles, and nighty-night cookies are on the dessert table.

It's not just Munder's jelly, crepes, and cookies that have been passed down through the generations. It is the importance she placed on gathering as a family, having meaningful conversations, using every activity as an opportunity for connection, and sharing the Christian faith. While our festivities usually involved food, decorations, and presents, the Lord was at the center of our celebrations. This is what tradition can do.

Certain holidays and traditions were instituted by God himself. In the Old Testament, he established several annual holidays for celebration, fellowship, and worship. He placed the Passover, the Festival of Unleavened Bread, the Offering of Firstfruits, the Festival of Weeks, the Festival of Trumpets, the Festival of Tabernacles, and the Day of Atonement on Israel's calendar (Leviticus 23; Numbers 28–29). These holidays provided a time for the Israelites to refresh themselves and renew their commitment to God. During these feasts, family members of all ages were reminded of his work in their lives. But tradition for tradition's sake is just another ritual. The true heart of these traditions is connection to God and those around us.

This was true in biblical times, and it is still true today. Holidays and traditions are annual reminders of what God has done, and they give us opportunities to connect to others. It's important to develop traditions in our families to serve as reminders for the older people and learning experiences for the younger ones.

Do you have any traditions, special dates, activities, or places that help you commemorate significant events in your life? Especially those events where God has done something for you? While traditions often revolve around major events such as the birth and resurrection of Jesus, they can also serve to celebrate personal moments—the little things maybe only you would recognize, such as how God answered a certain prayer, supplied for your need, or made himself incredibly known to you.

As evidenced by Scripture, God cares about our connection with him and with others, and we can choose to continue time-honored traditions. Think about what heritage you want to give to your family and the significance your customs carry. How can you tell others of God's faithfulness by creating a new tradition of your own or by continuing a tradition that was passed on to you? Whatever traditions you and I practice, I pray they are rooted in biblical truth and keep God at the forefront so future generations can connect with him and connect with each other. Because if there is anything worth passing on, it is him.

Your Little Task

What is your favorite tradition? Be intentional about connecting to God and others as you commemorate these special occasions.

Prayer Prompt

Lord, thank you for creating traditions and holidays to commemorate special events. You are worthy of our celebration. May I keep your traditions alive so future generations will know of your greatness as well as your goodness. Amen.

A Little Gesture

Then Mary took about a pint of pure nard, an expensive perfume;
she poured it on Jesus' feet and wiped his feet with her hair. And the
house was filled with the fragrance of the perfume.

JOHN 12:3

The wet drops on my head confirmed my fears. Dark clouds had
been threatening throughout my walk, and now, far from home
and without rain gear, I resigned myself to the fact that I was going
to get soaked.

Head down, I forged ahead on the muddy path. As I
rounded a bend, I caught a glimpse of two rain boot–clad children
holding two umbrellas—one opened above my children covering
them, and one extended in love to cover me.

"We heard the rain and didn't want you to get wet," my
children said.

Though my clothes were drenched and my fingertips tingled
with cold, my heart was warmed by their selfless love. Their gesture was simple, yet I was profoundly impacted by their willingness to lay aside their own desire to stay warm and dry to meet me
in my need. It was such a small gesture but one with lasting effects
on my heart.

In the Gospel of John, we read about Mary, who offered a
simple, yet sacrificial gesture to Jesus. Mary was a friend of Jesus
and the sister of Lazarus and Martha. In chapter 12, the friends
were having dinner in Bethany. Jesus was reclining at the table,
and Mary approached him with an alabaster jar of very expensive

perfume. This perfume was made of pure nard, a fragrant ointment imported from the mountains of India. While Mary must have known its value, she willingly broke the jar and poured the perfume on Jesus' feet and wiped his feet with her hair. What a beautiful moment between Jesus and Mary.

Others present must have also known its value because they called her offering a waste. They were angry and rebuked her, saying the perfume could have been sold for more than a year's wages and the money given to the poor (12:5–6). In response to their indignation, Jesus said, "Leave her alone…It was intended that she should save this perfume for the day of my burial. You will always have the poor among you, but you will not always have me" (12:7–8).

Of the disciples who were disgruntled at dinner, Judas Iscariot was especially angry. He specifically was the one who rebuked Mary (12:4–5). His resentment over Mary's gesture was based in greed rather than concern for the poor. As the treasurer of Jesus' ministry, Judas likely wanted to sell the perfume so he could embezzle the proceeds.

His reaction is in stark contrast to Mary's devotion to Jesus, shown through her unselfish gesture. In most situations, we can choose to be a Judas or a Mary. Will we act selfishly with devotion toward ourselves or unselfishly with devotion to Jesus and the people in our lives? When we choose the latter, we willingly sacrifice what is most precious to us for the benefit of others.

What I love most about this story is that Jesus appreciated Mary's gesture. I believe he appreciates our gestures, too, when we offer them with pure motives. I pray that, like Mary, we make a habit of sitting at Jesus' feet (Luke 10:39). And as she learned, sitting at his feet compels us toward thoughtfulness and unselfishness to cover others in his love. I think Jesus would call that a beautiful thing.

Your Little Task

Set aside an umbrella. The next time it's raining and you see someone without an umbrella, give them yours.

Prayer Prompt

*Lord, forgive me for the times I have acted selfishly.
Change my heart to think about how I can offer
you and others what I have. I will do my best and
let you take care of the rest. I pray that all I do is a
fragrant offering to you. Amen.*

A Little Letter

You yourselves are our letter, written on our hearts, known and read by everyone. You show that you are a letter from Christ, the result of our ministry, written not with ink but with the Spirit of the living God, not on tablets of stone but on tablets of human hearts.

2 CORINTHIANS 3:2–3

I was having a rough day but didn't have the time to work through my raw emotions. My feelings would have to wait because I had an interview in fifteen minutes, and I needed to push through. As I walked into my office, I immediately noticed a card propped on top of my computer. I removed the card from the envelope to find a note from my mom. Moments before receiving her letter, tears threatened to fall due to frustration and hurt, but now they fell in comfort and gratitude as I read her thoughtful words. My mom's simple letter helped me regroup minutes before my interview. What impeccable timing.

This wasn't the first impactful letter or note from my mom. I have a memory box full of holiday cards, lunch box notes, and words of wisdom she has mailed to me to mark various milestones in my life. I imagine you have received handwritten letters over the years that you treasure as well—keeping them safely tucked away to read again and again.

I like to think of the Bible in the same way—as God's love letter to me filled with wisdom and encouragement to refer back to again and again. His words meet me right where I am every time I open the Bible, and they serve as a reminder of his presence in my life.

While the Old Testament and the Gospels contain treasures of their own, the New Testament also contains epistles. The word *epistle* comes from the Greek word *epistolé*, which means "letter." These letters make up the majority of the New Testament. Of the twenty-seven New Testament books, twenty-one are epistles.

One epistle was written as a personal letter to a single individual (Philemon). The others were written to churches in specific cities or to the universal church made up of believers who never personally met Jesus. Most of the epistles were written by the apostle Paul. He is thought to have written thirteen of them. The apostles Peter, John, James, and Jude wrote the rest.

Just like the early church, the epistles are valuable to us because they show us what it means to follow Jesus in practical, everyday, authentic ways without having Jesus physically present. The apostles were able to reach hundreds and thousands through their original letters. Two thousand years later, they are still a gift to all who read them. I doubt the apostles ever dreamed the words they penned through the inspiration of the Holy Spirit would reach millions more. Could our letters do the same one day?

But it's not just our letters written with paper and ink that can make a difference. Paul says, "You yourselves are our letter, written on our hearts, known and read by everyone. You show that you are a letter from Christ, the result of our ministry, written not with ink but with the Spirit of the living God, not on tablets of stone but on tablets of human hearts" (2 Corinthians 3:2–3). Sweet sister, this is my letter of encouragement to you and a reminder to me as well. May our lives prove that God is the author and that he alone holds the pen. Let him supply the words—you just be obedient to write them.

Your Little Task

Write a letter to someone whom God places on your heart.
Prayerfully consider what God might have you say to them.

Prayer Prompt

*Lord, thank you for communicating, encouraging,
inspiring, convicting, and teaching me through
your Word. I treasure it. I am grateful for the
apostles' willingness to write the epistles, which I
am impacted by today. May I also listen to your
voice and be sensitive to whomever you put on my
heart. I trust you will take the words on the page
and bless the recipient now and for years to come.
Amen.*

A Little Courage

For the Spirit God gave us does not make us timid,
but gives us power, love and self-discipline.

2 TIMOTHY 1:7

"Mom, I'm scared," Kate whispered as she reached for my hand. We were on a girls' trip in Savannah, Georgia, where oak trees draped with Spanish moss lined the cobblestone streets and notable historic buildings told the story of this charming port city. We were exploring the city together for the first time, and the unfamiliar setting made Kate nervous.

But, as we made our way back to our hotel that evening, Kate was smiling. She was happy about the excursion and delighted that she had faced her fear. I was so proud of her for being courageous even when she felt afraid, and I was thankful that she hadn't let her discomfort stop us from enjoying a day full of souvenirs, sweets, and a sunset.

As I reflect on this experience, I can't help but wonder how often we allow fear to rule and keep us from experiencing what God may have for us or what he wants to accomplish through us. While we often face more difficult circumstances in life than navigating a new city, the lesson remains the same: fear can stop us from experiencing joy and realizing God-given plans, but if we courageously push forward despite fear, amazing things can happen.

In Exodus, we meet a group of women who, despite their fear, acted with courage. The story begins in chapter one as

Pharaoh issues an edict for the Hebrew midwives to kill all of the baby boys. The midwives disobeyed Pharaoh's orders and spared the babies. Their conviction and faith in God gave them the courage to take a stand for what they knew was right despite the potential personal consequences they might have to endure.

Another woman willing to trust in the Lord above man was Jochebed. She knew how wrong it would be to destroy her child, but there was little she could do to change Pharoah's law. Her only alternative was to hide the baby. Keeping a baby quiet for three months was no small task. When she could hide him no longer, she placed him in a tiny papyrus basket on the Nile River. I can't imagine how she felt placing him in the water that day, trusting God to care for him. How her heart must have broken.

The baby's older sister, Miriam, acted bravely as well. That day, she stood along the river to see what would happen to her brother. When she saw that the Pharaoh's daughter discovered the baby, she quickly took the initiative to suggest a nurse (her mother) to care for him. The princess agreed to Miriam's proposal, which resulted in Jochebed's family being reunited. When the child grew older, Jochebed took him to Pharaoh's daughter. He became her son, and she named him Moses.

You may know the rest of Moses' story. God used him to rescue his people from slavery in Egypt. Through him we also get the Ten Commandments. But what if the midwives, Jochebed, Miriam, and Pharaoh's daughter hadn't rescued him first? They had no way of knowing the effect their courage would have eighty years later. Had they not acted with such bravery, history as we know it would have been altered.

Like Moses and the women who cared for him, God has special opportunities for us too. However, if we let the fear of what might happen rule us, we will live with a lifetime of regret. We can act with courage because we know God is with us. Just as Kate reached for my hand for strength, we must choose to cling to God in order to overcome our fears and live bravely.

What is God asking you to do? Is there a risk he is asking you to take? Even as you whisper, "God, I'm scared," he will be with you to hold your hand every step of the way—all the way to the streets of gold.

Your Little Task

Next time you are faced with a fear, reach out for the hand of the Lord and let him guide you forward in faith.

Prayer Prompt

Lord, you make me brave. I know your perfect love casts out fear. Give me the wisdom to know when to take a step and when to stay still. I trust in your provision and protection as I obey your promptings. Help me to sense your presence and peace as I act with courage. Amen.

A Little Thought

Finally, brothers and sisters, whatever is true, whatever is noble,
whatever is right, whatever is pure, whatever is lovely,
whatever is admirable—if anything is excellent or praiseworthy—
think about such things.

PHILIPPIANS 4:8

Whenever I ask a friend of mine how she is, she always responds by saying, "I'm amazing!" The first time Hannah answered this way, I literally laughed because it was so unexpected. Usually, people respond with "I'm okay," or "I'm fine," whether they really are or not, so her reply took me by surprise. When I pressed her as to why she was so amazing, Hannah explained that it was her way of giving herself a positive affirmation. She said if she tells others she's amazing, she starts to believe it too. Alternatively, if Hannah's inner narrative and response was, "I'm a failure," she might actually start feeling like a failure and hence acting like a failure. This would then reinforce the belief that she was a failure because what we think directly influences how we feel and how we behave.

I did a bit of research, and I discovered that the average person has approximately twelve thousand to sixty thousand thoughts per day.[2] Of those thousands of thoughts, 80 percent are negative, and 95 percent are exactly the same repetitive thoughts as the day before. Isn't this disheartening? I also discovered that our brains

---

[2]   Neringa Antanaityte, "Mind Matters: How to Effortlessly Have More Positive Thoughts," TLEX Institute (website), accessed August 14, 2021, https://tlexinstitute.com/how-to-effortlessly-have-more-positive-thoughts/.

are made up of an estimated one hundred billion neurons making a total of one hundred trillion neural connections.[3] Our goal then should be to use these connections constructively—to shift our thought lives to be 100 percent positive. Wouldn't that be life changing?

Thankfully, scientists have proven that it is possible to alter our brains through a process known as *neuroplasticity*.[4] Essentially, neuroplasticity is our brain's ability to be shaped by our everyday experiences. Here is a simple way to understand how it works: just as a path becomes flattened every time a person walks over it, as we focus on something with our thoughts, feelings, and behaviors, we strengthen our brain pathways. Over days, months, and years, a frequently traveled trail becomes a well-worn pathway. This is why the habits we've had for many years are the most challenging to change. They have carved ruts in our brains. The good news is we can change our brains by intentionally creating new positive pathways.

This scientific research is validated by Scripture in the writings of Paul from thousands of years ago. In the book of Romans, he teaches us to "be transformed by the renewing of [our minds]" (Romans 12:2). The Contemporary English Version of this verse says, "to let God change the way you think." The transformation of our minds is the work of the Holy Spirit in our lives, but it also happens through our intentionality. We have to deliberately fill our minds with positive thoughts because what we consume becomes our inner narrative. If we don't saturate ourselves in the truth from

---

3   "Neural Plasticity: 4 Steps to Change Your Brain and Habits," Authenticity Associates (website), June 21, 2010, https://www.authenticityassociates.com/neural-plasticity-4-steps-to-change-your-brain/.

4   "Neuroplasticity," Wikipedia (website), last edited October 20, 2021, https://en.wikipedia.org/wiki/Neuroplasticity.

God's Word, lies and negative affirmations begin to crowd our minds instead.

Paul tells us to program our minds with thoughts that are true, noble, right, pure, lovely, admirable, excellent, and praise-worthy (Philippians 4:8). Yet, how often do we think on things that are false, dishonorable, wrong, impure, ugly, detestable, unexceptional, and unworthy? I know I'm guilty of these thought cycles, but Philippians 4:8 is the litmus test we need to filter every thought through.

It's time to take our thoughts more seriously. In the words of an ancient Chinese proverb by Lao Tzu, "Watch your thoughts, they become your words; watch your words, they become your actions; watch your actions, they become your habits; watch your habits, they become your character; watch your character, it becomes your destiny."[5] There is so much at stake, and to think, it all starts in our minds.

PS: I think you're amazing!

Your Little Task

Pay attention to your thoughts. Catch any negative thought and replace it with a truth from Scripture.

---

[5] "Quote by Lao Tzu," Goodreads (website), Goodreads Inc., accessed November 1, 2021, https://www.goodreads.com/quotes/8203490-watch-your-thoughts-they-become-your-words-watch-your-words.

*Lord, you have searched me, and you know me.
You know when I sit and when I rise; you perceive
my thoughts from afar (Psalm 139:1–2). How
precious to me are your thoughts, O God! How
vast is the sum of them! Search me, O God, and
know my heart; test me and know my anxious
thoughts. See if there is any offensive way in me,
and lead me in the way everlasting. Thank you for
creating my mind. Fill it with your truth. May I
meditate on your Word alone to renew my mind
day by day. Amen.*

A Little Clothing

"I needed clothes and you clothed me."
MATTHEW 25:36

Every year, the family resource teachers in our county join together to organize an event called the Princess Prom Project. These ladies gather donated dresses, shoes, purses, and jewelry and display them in a local church gym. After, the dresses are hung by size and color. Girls who could otherwise not afford to attend prom are invited to come shop. Volunteers serve as personal shoppers for the teenagers, joining them in their dressing rooms to zip dresses and help them decide on the perfect gown. Once the young ladies are happy with their selections, they are ushered to another corner of the gym to have their dresses altered. There, a group of seamstresses pin, sew, and steam each girl's ensemble until it is as if it were tailor-made for her. Several weekends later, on the day of the prom, the young ladies return to complete the full princess treatment, which includes getting their nails, hair, and makeup done, as well as being photographed.

One year, I had the opportunity to serve in hospitality for this event. My job was to stay with the princesses as they moved from station to station, ensuring they were never lacking refreshment, conversation, or laughter.

Throughout both weekends, I heard some of the stories of these young ladies—many of them heartbreaking. But I also witnessed their smiles as they got to be the center of attention and feel beautiful because of the special treatment they received. I wish

I could have been a fly on the wall that night at prom to see them dance.

My heart fills with joy as I think about their attire and the princesses who wore the dresses first then generously donated them so these other young women could feel like princesses too. I'm curious what will happen to the dresses now that the dance is over. Will they be donated again so other young women can one day dance with joy?

A disciple named Tabitha is a great example of a woman who ministered to others in this way. She was a part of the first church in Acts. Luke, the author of the book, tells us Tabitha was always doing good and helping the poor. When she died, the community sent for Peter to pray for her. He arrived to see a room filled with mourners. All the town widows showed him the robes and other clothing Tabitha had made while she was still with them. Seeing their distress, Peter prayed for Tabitha, and she miraculously opened her eyes and sat up. This miracle became known all over their community, and as a result, many people believed in the Lord (Acts 9).

Reflecting on Tabitha's story, I doubt she would have been loved and mourned to such an extent if she had not tangibly loved the poor by making clothes for them. Had they not loved her so much, they probably would not have called Peter to pray for her. Had he not prayed for her healing, many in the community wouldn't have been saved. And to think, their salvation started with something so little—a simple piece of clothing!

Your Little Task.

Look for opportunities to share your clothing with others by donating or simply letting them borrow something for an occasion.

Prayer Prompt

Lord, help me not to worry about the clothes I will wear and, instead, trust that you will clothe me. More than the outer clothes I wear, clothe me with a heart of compassion and kindness. When I see someone in need of clothing, remind me of your words, "I needed clothes and you clothed me" (Matthew 25:36). Make this my heart, and may my actions follow suit. Amen.

A Little Gratitude

Let the message of Christ dwell among you richly as you teach and
admonish one another with all the wisdom through psalms, hymns,
and songs from the Spirit, singing to God with gratitude in your
hearts. And whatever you do, whether in word or deed, do it all in the
name of the Lord Jesus, giving thanks to God the Father through him.
COLOSSIANS 3:16–17

Through my car window, I saw him slouching against the pizza
parlor wall. His clothes were tattered and dirty. Beside him, stuffed
into a grocery sack, was what appeared to be all of his belongings.
Moved with compassion, I ordered an extra pizza and drink.

When I approached him to give him dinner, he took the
pizza from me and then proceeded to throw it at me. Instead of
being met with gratitude, I was met with anger. I walked away in
disbelief, questioning why God had prompted me to be generous
to someone who was so unappreciative.

Has your giving ever been met with an ungrateful heart?
Not only can I relate, but Jesus can too. He noticed the ungrateful
spirit of those with whom he came into contact. This was the case
when he healed ten men with leprosy. One of them, when he was
healed, came back and praised God. He threw himself at Jesus' feet
and thanked him (Luke 17:11–16).

"Jesus asked, 'Were not all ten cleansed? Where are the
other nine? Has no one returned to give praise to God except this
foreigner?' Then he said to him, 'Rise and go; your faith has made
you well'" (Luke 17:17–19). Isn't it unthinkable that nine of these

men received God's gift and never thanked him? One out of ten is not a good ratio.

Let's put ourselves into this story and imagine for a moment that we are the ten lepers. Upon introspection, are we like the nine who have received God's great gifts with an ungrateful heart, or are we like the one who reacted gratefully? While God does not demand that we thank him, through this teaching, we learn that he is pleased when we do so. All ten men received healing, but only the thankful man learned that his faith had played a role in the process. As we react with gratitude, Jesus uses our responsiveness to teach us more about himself as well.

Just as Jesus gave even when gratitude was not guaranteed, the gratitude of others is not a prerequisite or expectation for our giving. However, it is nice when we are appreciated, isn't it?

The apparent ungratefulness of the man at the pizza parlor is rare. Honestly, my heart is still moved with compassion for this man. His reaction to me revealed his true desperation. More often than not, when I give to others, I am met with thankfulness. There aren't enough pages in this devotional to record all of the times I have been blessed by giving.

I tell this story because I think it's important to remember that we aren't giving to others for the reaction we get. It isn't about reciprocity from people; it is about our reverence for God. We are simply to be obedient, remembering that Jesus said, "Whatever you did for one of the least of these…you did for me" (Matthew 25:40). Everything we do for him is out of gratitude for what he has done for us. And even more so, out of gratitude for who he is.

When someone does something for you or says something kind, say thank you. Perhaps it's even the Lord you need to thank.

Lord, help me to give thanks to you in every circumstance. Forgive me for the times I've had an ungrateful heart. I am thankful for everything you have given me and for who you are. May I not only react with gratitude for what others do for me but also simply for who they are. I pray I give to others out of my gratitude for you, regardless of how they respond to me. Amen.

A Little Encouragement

Therefore encourage one another and build each other up,
just as in fact you are doing.
1 THESSALONIANS 5:11

I ran a half-marathon once. About halfway through the course
was a steep and long hill. My feet and lungs were begging me to
stop when suddenly my friends and family came into view. They
were smiling, clapping, cheering, and holding signs with uplift-
ing quotes on them, and their support gave me the strength to
continue. Their kindness met me each mile along the course and
continued to encourage me all the way to the finish.

A little word of encouragement offered at the right moment
can be the difference between finishing well and collapsing along the
way, can't it? In our everyday lives, simple heartfelt words can make
such a significant impact on our strength and ability to carry on.

Words like:

- I love you.
- I'm thinking of you.
- I miss you.
- How are you?
- You can do this!
- I admire you.
- You're beautiful.
- You are talented.
- You make me happy.

- Your work is impressive!
- I'm so glad God put you in my life.

Oh, what a difference a thoughtful text, a courteous call, or a love-filled letter can make, especially on days when we are feeling emotionally worn or distressed.

We find a beautiful example of this kind of encouragement from a man named Barnabas. Nicknamed "the Son of Encouragement," Barnabas quietly influenced Christianity. His actions were crucial to the early church, and God used his relationship with Paul and Mark to keep these two men going to fulfill God's calling.

When Paul arrived in Jerusalem for the first time following his conversion, the local Christians were understandably reluctant to welcome him. But Barnabas proved willing to risk his life to meet with Paul and then convince others that their former enemy was now a believer in Jesus (Acts 9:26–28). Eventually, these men set off on a missionary journey together. Mark later joined Paul and Barnabas as their assistant. At their second stop, Mark left them and returned to Jerusalem. It was a decision Paul did not easily accept. In preparing for their second journey two years later, Barnabas again suggested Mark as a traveling companion, but Paul refused. As a result, the team was divided—Barnabas took Mark with him while Paul chose Silas (Acts 15:36–40). Barnabas' patient encouragement helped Mark stay the course, and later, Paul and Mark were reunited. The older apostle even became a close friend of the young disciple (2 Timothy 4:11).

Thinking about this makes me wonder: What if Barnabas hadn't encouraged these men? If Paul had been discouraged and given up, would he have written all the letters of the New Testament we are able to read today? The same is true of Mark. If he had walked away, we wouldn't have the Gospel of Mark. Barnabas refreshed these men so they could then go on to refresh others.

How about us? Are our words a refreshing influence on others or a discouragement?

Scripture says, "The mouth speaks what the heart is full of" (Matthew 12:34), and our words can bring either life or death (Proverbs 18:21). Therefore, in order to share words that uplift rather than tear down, we must be intentional about filling our hearts with God's Word. And, on occasions when we don't know what to say to encourage the people in our lives, we can always use God's words found in the Bible.

We are all running this marathon of life. On the flat stretches, downgrades, and especially those steep uphill climbs, your words of encouragement could be what keeps your fellow runner going. May we all finish well, encouraging each other every step of the way, knowing there is a great crowd of witnesses cheering us on as we do (Hebrews 12:1).

Your Little Task

Make a list of your favorite encouraging phrases. Feel free to look at the examples I offered. Then share your encouragement with someone whom God places on your heart.

Lord, thank you for everyone you have placed in my life who has been an encouragement to me. Most of all, thank you for your Word and its constant encouragement. Fill me with your truth so that what is in my heart is only what you would have me to speak. Open my eyes to those around me who may need a word of encouragement. Give me the words to share and help me to be obedient to share them. Amen.

A Little Story

Then Philip ran up to the chariot and heard the man reading Isaiah the prophet. "Do you understand what you are reading?" Philip asked. "How can I," he said, "unless someone explains it to me?" So he invited Philip to come up and sit with him.

ACTS 8:30–31

Every day after school, my son Will's coach reads a devotion to the team before they practice or play a game. One day, his coach told the players that if any of them wanted one of the devotionals he was reading from he would be happy to purchase one for them. Will asked for a copy, and his coach followed through and bought a devotional for him.

I didn't know about his coach's gesture until I found the devotional in Will's backpack at the end of the day. When I asked Will if he would like to keep it in his backpack or put it on his nightstand, Will said that he wanted to keep it in his backpack so he could read it at school. He said that his teacher gives them fifteen minutes of free reading, and he wanted to read his new devotional during that time.

I'm excited to see what God does in his heart through the reading of Scripture. I'm also excited at the possibility of his other classmates seeing what Will is reading and asking questions about the content. And I'm even more excited about the possibility that seeing Will reading God's story might inspire someone else in his class to begin reading their own Bible or devotional.

In the book of Acts, we find an account that shows the kind of impact reading a story can have. The passage begins by introducing us to Phillip, who was preaching and ministering to great crowds. However, God asked him to leave that ministry to travel the desert road. I imagine he must have wondered why God would remove him from a setting where he was obviously having a significant influence in order to travel a road with conceivably no one on it. To his human eyes, God's direction wouldn't have made sense or might have felt like a demotion, but as we keep reading, we discover why it mattered.

Along the road, Phillip met an Ethiopian who was trying to read the Bible. "'Do you understand what you are reading?' Philip asked. 'How can I,' he said, 'unless someone explains it to me?'" So he invited Philip to sit with him and read. At that moment, Philip wouldn't have known the impact this would make. However, we now know that Philip's reading to the Ethiopian and sharing the gospel with this man helped him come to Christ. And, because the Ethiopian was an important official, Philip's actions helped place a Christian in a significant position in a distant country, which may have had an effect on the entire nation. In fact, the Ethiopian might have been the first witness to the ends of the earth (Acts 8).

As I think about the example and leadership set by Will's coach by doing something so simple as reading a five-minute daily devotion to his team, it causes me to think about the impact of a story. Who first read the story of God to him? Was it his parents or possibly one of his coaches? Regardless of who first told it or how he first heard it, the important thing is that the story continues to be retold and explained—especially when that story is God's.

Share a story from the Bible with someone else. Talk about how God is speaking to you through the Scriptures.

Lord, thank you for your Word. Give me a hunger to read it and a desire to retell it. I'm so grateful for the people who shared it with me, and I pray I have the courage and compassion to share it with others. Amen.

Day 40

A Little Interruption

When Jesus heard what had happened, he withdrew by boat
privately to a solitary place. Hearing of this, the crowds followed him
on foot from the towns. When Jesus landed and saw the large crowd,
he had compassion on them and healed their sick.

MATTHEW 14:13–14

I had a deadline looming, and having finally found some space
on my calendar to devote to the project, I went to a coffee shop to
work. There, I nestled into a leather chair, took a sip of my nonfat
latte with a sprinkle of cinnamon, and, with a deep exhale, opened
my computer to begin.

Just as my fingers touched the keys, I spotted an acquaintance out of the corner of my eye. Panic rose in me. *I should have*
known better than to come to a public place to work, I thought. My
first impulse was to look away and reach for my earbuds, hoping
she hadn't noticed me or that, if she had, she would recognize that
I was busy. But after the initial feeling of panic, I felt a pang of conviction. So instead of looking busy, I looked up, took my hands off
the keyboard, and waved. My simple wave was the invitation she
needed to come over and settle into the chair beside me.

Two hours later, after laughter and a few tears, she stood to
leave. "I'm so thankful God let me run into you today. He must
have known I needed this," she said, hugging me goodbye.

At that moment, I was thankful too—thankful I had chosen to put a person in front of a project. I continue to be thankful
because my acquaintance has turned into a friend. One reluctant

impromptu conversation has led to ongoing scheduled coffee dates. God knew what he was doing when he interrupted me that day.

Interruptions can be frustrating. We all have things we want to do and things that need to get done, so we don't like anything that gets in the way of those plans. But what would happen if we changed our perspective to see interruptions as opportunities to embrace God's plan rather than obstacles to our agendas?

After all, the Gospels are full of interruptions to Jesus' schedule. Oftentimes, he was going somewhere when someone would stop him, giving him the opportunity to do something miraculous. I marvel at how he handled these interruptions. In Mark 5, Jesus was on his way to speak to a waiting crowd. As he was walking, a leader in the synagogue named Jairus came to ask Jesus to save his dying daughter. Jesus left the crowd to go with him. But, on the way to Jairus' house, a woman who had been bleeding for twelve years touched his robe. Jesus took time to talk with her and heal her suffering. While Jesus was still speaking, some men came from the house of Jairus to tell Jesus that the girl had died. Jesus continued on to Jairus' house anyway, and when he finally arrived, he took the girl by the hand and told her to get up. The girl came back to life, stood up, and walked around.

Just thinking about this series of events makes me feel anxious—being interrupted while a dying girl is waiting for me sounds incredibly stressful. But Jesus rose to each occasion. He always stopped what he was doing and focused on the person who interrupted him.

On another occasion, Jesus was interrupted while trying to meet his own needs. After finding out about John the Baptist's beheading, Jesus needed solitude. So, he got into a boat to spend time alone. However, a large crowd discovered his plan and waited for him on the other side of the lake. As Jesus' boat floated near the shore and he saw the crowd, I wonder what he thought and felt. I would have been frustrated at the sight and been tempted to stay in the boat or paddle in another direction. But Jesus didn't respond in any of these ways. He didn't feel frustrated; he felt compassion (Matthew 14:1–14).

Oh, how I want to respond in the same way. I want to see each interruption as a divine appointment from God instead of an irritation to me. I don't want to be so busy with projects that I have no time for people. Though interruptions catch me off guard, they do not catch God off guard. They are not meaningless events; rather, they are divinely placed in my path for a reason. I pray we lay aside our agendas and exchange our plans for his because the next interruption is likely an opportunity to be a part of his eternal plan.

Your Little Task

How do you see people who interrupt your schedule? As annoyances or as the reason for your life and ministry? The next time you are interrupted, take the time to stop and give the person your full attention. It very well could be a divine interruption.

Prayer Prompt

Lord, I trust in your plan and providence over my life. Forgive me for the times I have reacted with frustration when life doesn't go according to my plan. Give me eyes to see people and circumstances the way you do and a heart to respond the way you would. Help each interruption draw me closer to you and empower me to obey your promptings.
Amen.

A Little Perseverance

*Not only so, but we also glory in our sufferings, because we know
that suffering produces perseverance; perseverance, character;
and character, hope.*

ROMANS 5:3–4

Kate's first day of gymnastics did not go as planned. She expected
to have fun tumbling and making new friends, but instead, her
first class ended in tears of disappointment. The tumbling part had
gone fine, but making friends had not. In fact, no one had even
attempted to talk to her.

On the way home, I gave Kate examples of how to initiate
conversation, and we discussed a basic principle of friendship: to
have good friends, you have to be a good friend. However, since
she had just started the class, I told her we could try another class
on a different day or at a different time. If that didn't work, we
could try another gymnastics studio altogether. Or even quit if she
wanted. By the time we returned home, she still felt upset, but she
also felt reassured by the knowledge that she had options.

When I retold the story to Bryan that night at dinner, he
responded much differently than I had. "You can't quit already.
Push through and persevere. If you like gymnastics, keep at it, and
the friendships will come. Good relationships just take time," he
advised with tough love.

A wave of regret rose over me as I realized I'd given Kate
the wrong advice. I was tempted to take away the pain and let her
walk (or tumble) the easy road. But I'm learning what is easy is

not always what is best. Of course, there are situations when safety is at stake, but this wasn't one of those instances. Rather, it was an opportunity to develop character, confidence, and resilience in my daughter. She needed to learn to persevere through hard situations.

Goodness, I am still learning this lesson in adulthood. Aren't we tempted to quit when things get hard or uncomfortable? I wonder how many times in our lives we would have realized our dream, the desire of our hearts, or the call on our lives if we had pushed through just a little longer.

I think about the way many of the heroes of our faith persevered despite difficult or long-lasting circumstances. Consider how their stories would have changed if they had quit too soon. What if Moses had stopped pleading with Pharaoh after nine plagues rather than ten? The Israelites would have remained in slavery in Egypt. What if Joshua and the Israelites had stopped walking around the wall of Jericho after six times rather than seven? They would have never seen the walls fall and entered into the promised land. What if Noah had only built half of an ark? That would not have floated very well, would it? Nor would his family and all of those animals have lived through the flood. And what about you? What if you are on the brink of a breakthrough and stop too soon?

I don't know how long you have been circling the same problem or what difficult situation you are facing today, but if you are tempted to give up, I hope you will reconsider. I learned a valuable lesson through Kate's experience. Thankfully, she took her father's advice and went back to the same gym with the same girls—but now with a different result. Each week she falls down and gets back up again. I'm amazed at her athletic perseverance, but I'm even more amazed by her emotional perseverance. Slowly but surely, at each class she attends, she makes more and more friends. Had she taken my initial advice, she would have missed out on it all.

Let's not miss out on what God has for us by giving up too soon. When our Father doesn't change our current circumstance, it is likely he is giving us tough love because he wants to develop character, confidence, and resilience in us. No matter how hard it feels, when we fall down, I pray we get up, try again, and trust he has his hand extended to catch us.

Your Little Task

Get quiet with the Lord and ask him to reveal any areas or relationships you gave up on too soon. Resolve to finish what you started.

Prayer Prompt

Father, forgive me for the times I quit because the task felt too hard or was taking too long to complete. Give me strength and patient endurance to keep going even when I feel weary and am tempted to give up. I want to throw off everything that hinders and the sin that so easily entangles. Help me run with perseverance the race marked out for me. Amen.

A Little Seed

*"The kingdom of heaven is like a mustard seed, which a man took
and planted in his field. Though it is the smallest of all seeds, yet
when it grows, it is the largest of the garden plants and becomes a
tree, so that the birds come and perch in its branches."*

MATTHEW 13:31–32

When our family moved to a farm, we were pleasantly surprised
to find a raised garden bed filled with fruits and vegetables ripe for
picking. I was grateful for the time and care the previous owners
had taken to plant and water the garden. As the new owners, we
were able to enjoy the fruit of their labor.

The next spring, it was our turn to plant. As I dropped each
seed into the freshly turned dirt, I marveled at their various sizes
and shapes. Weeks later, I watched in wonder at the speed with
which they grew and the amount of food that stemmed from
something so small.

While the miraculous process of sowing seeds and reaping a
harvest was clearly displayed in my garden, it isn't always so obvi-
ous in our lives. Often, we do a good deed, such as praying for a
co-worker or spending time playing with a neighbor kid, and never
see the tangible results of our efforts. During a conversation with a
friend about the desire to see the fruit of our labor, she challenged
me with this thought: "Are you okay with being the one to plant
the seed and never see the harvest?" My fleshly answer was no, but
I know Scripture encourages me otherwise. In 1 Corinthians 3:6,
Paul said that he planted the seed and Apollos watered it, but God

made it grow. God is helping me learn to let go of my desire to see a visible outcome and to leave the harvest up to him.

In the Gospel of Matthew, Jesus also taught about sowing seeds. In the parable of the sower, a farmer was scattering seed. The parable says:

> Some fell along the path, and the birds came and ate it up. Some fell on rocky places…[and] sprang up quickly, because the soil was shallow. But when the sun came up, the plants were scorched, and they withered because they had no root. Other seed fell among thorns, which grew up and choked the plants. Still other seed fell on good soil, where it produced a crop—a hundred, sixty or thirty times what was sown. (Matthew 13:1–9)

The farmer knew some soil was good and some was not, so he threw the seed liberally enough that the good ground would ensure a plentiful harvest. Even so, the yield wasn't dependent on the farmer. It was dependent on the condition of the soil where the seed fell. The four soils represent the ways people respond to God's message, but regardless of how they respond, it is our responsibility to keep sowing the seed.

Jesus told another parable related to sowing in faith. He said, "The kingdom of heaven is like a mustard seed, which a man took and planted in his field. Though it is the smallest of all seeds, yet when it grows, it is the largest of the garden plants and becomes a tree, so that the birds come and perch in its branches" (Matthew 13:31–32).

The mustard seed is one of the tiniest seeds found in the Middle East, yet it is a fast-growing annual herb that grows up to ten feet tall in just a few short months. Jesus used this parable to show how his kingdom appeared to have small beginnings but would grow into a worldwide community of believers.

We are already seeing his parable come to fruition. However, there are more seeds to be sown. While our efforts may seem small and we don't always see the fruit of our labor, it's important to remember that God is at work. Keep your eyes on the great harvest to come. Continue liberally sowing seeds no matter how small they seem and trust God to help them grow. Who knows who will end up benefiting from the fruit of your labor!

Your Little Task

Plant a seed and watch it grow as a daily reminder of God's work in you.

Prayer Prompt

Lord, thank you for those who have planted and watered seeds in my life. Help my heart to be full of fertile soil. May I be deeply rooted in you. Give me faith to keep planting seeds in the lives of others regardless of whether or not I see the fruit. Remind me that the harvest is plenty, but the workers are few. Amen.

A Little Kindness

"May I continue to find favor in your eyes, my lord," she said.
"You have put me at ease by speaking kindly to your servant—
though I do not have the standing of one of your servants."

RUTH 2:13

Until the contractor could start building our home, our plan was to build a barn where our family could live in the interim. With our move-out date looming, time was of the essence for construction of the barn to begin. I was ecstatic when my husband, Bryan, sent me a picture of the trusses that had just been installed. Only two hours later, I received another text from him, this one saying that the barn had just been destroyed by a tornado-like storm that blew through the land. Our future home was in shambles.

As friends and family heard about the natural disaster and our resulting predicament, they extended kindness to us in some way or another. Some offered their basements for us to live in, others offered their RVs or rental homes, others offered their hands or tools to help rebuild, and most all of them offered their encouraging words and prayers. Luckily, we never had to take them up on their offers, aside from their kind words and prayers, of course. However, as tough of a blow (literally) as this time was, I'll never forget our community's kindness as they rallied around us. We need the kindness of others all the time, but we especially need it in the trying times, don't we?

We find a beautiful example of kindness in the book of Ruth. As widows, Ruth and Naomi were in desperate need, and God, in his kindness, directed the women to Naomi's relative named Boaz. When Ruth went to Boaz's fields to pick up leftover grain, he noticed Ruth and told her she could stay to work, eat, and drink on his land. However, Boaz went far beyond the intent of the gleaner's law. Not only did he let Ruth glean in his field, but he also told his workers to let some of the grain fall in her path. Ruth was overcome by his kindness (2:13), and when Naomi heard all that had transpired that day, she marveled at his kindness too (2:20).

One day, Naomi suggested that Ruth lay at Boaz's feet on the threshing floor. When he noticed her, Boaz was blessed Ruth chose him, rather than a younger man, to be her kinsman-redeemer. This term *kinsman-redeemer* refers to a relative who volunteers to take responsibility for extended family. In those days, when a woman's husband died, the law provided that she could marry a brother of her dead husband. But Naomi had no more sons. In such a case, the nearest relative of the deceased husband could become a kinsman-redeemer and marry the widow. However, the nearest relative did not have to marry the widow. If he chose not to, the next nearest relative could take his place. If no one chose to help the widow, she would likely live in poverty the rest of her life because, in the Israelite culture, inheritance was passed on to the son or nearest male relative, not to the wife.

This is why Ruth was overwhelmed by Boaz's kindness when he agreed to step in as her kinsman-redeemer. To make it official and legal, he went to the town gate to confirm with the elders that he could become her guardian and purchase her property. Ruth became his wife, and she gave birth to a son. They named him Obed. Obed became the father of Jesse and the grandfather of David, members of the genealogy of Jesus.

Jesus is our kinsman-redeemer. He came to the earth as a man in order to save us. Without him, our lives are in shambles, and we are left with the destruction life can bring. He knew we would have trying times, so in the ultimate act of kindness, he died for us on the cross to redeem us from sin and hopelessness and to purchase us as his own possession. This guarantees our eternal inheritance—a kindness I pray you and I never forget.

Your Little Task

Look around to see how you might be able to show kindness to others. Choose one little act of kindness that would be significant to someone God puts on your heart.

Prayer Prompt

Lord, I can never repay your kindness, and I'm grateful you don't expect me to. Allow me to recognize and appreciate the kindness of others to me. I know this attribute is a fruit of your Spirit, so help me be sensitive to the needs of those around me and be kind. Amen.

A Little Look

Nothing in all creation is hidden from God's sight.
HEBREWS 4:13

My friend Jill and I were discussing how we feel hurt and over-looked when others don't look us in the eyes. The topic of conversation caused Jill to recount a story from her trip to a large city. She recalled walking along a busy street and noticing a homeless man sitting on the sidewalk. Listening to the Holy Spirit's prompting, Jill intentionally looked the man in the eyes as she passed him.

Locking eyes with her, the man questioned in disbelief, "Do you see me?"

"Yes, I see you," she responded.

"No one ever sees me," he replied.

Doesn't his statement hurt your heart? How long had it been since someone had looked his way? It's challenging to think about how merely making eye contact made an impact and helped this man feel valued and loved. What a simple gesture, yet how often do we turn our eyes away instead?

In the book of Acts, Peter and John were heading to the temple courts when they saw someone who was always over-looked. A lame man was being carried to the temple courts, where he was taken every day to beg. When he saw Peter and John, he asked them for money. They didn't ignore him or give a sideways glance and walk by. Instead, Peter and John looked straight at the man and said, "Look at us." The lame man gave them his attention, expecting to get something from them. Peter told the man, "Silver or gold I do not have, but what I do have I give you. In the name of Jesus Christ of Nazareth, walk" (Acts 3:6). Immediately the man was transformed from lame and hopeless to jumping and praising God. When the townspeople saw the beggar now healed, they, too, were filled with wonder and amazement.

Before this interaction, Peter had already learned the value of a look. He was taught this lesson when he and the other disciples were crossing the Sea of Galilee and got caught in a storm. In the midst of the wind and waves, they saw Jesus walking on the water, and Peter asked if he could join him. At Jesus' invitation, Peter stepped out of the boat and, miraculously, walked on water—until he took his eyes off Jesus, at which point he started to sink. Luckily, Jesus never took his eyes off him because he reached out, grabbed Peter's arm, and helped him back into the boat (Matthew 14:22–32).

Friend, we also need to keep our eyes fixed on the Lord, and we can take great comfort in knowing his eyes are fixed on us too. Scripture tells us, "The eyes of the LORD are everywhere" (Proverbs 15:3) and that he looks down from heaven and sees all of mankind (Psalm 33:13). Nothing in all creation is hidden from his sight (Hebrews 4:13) because he is *El Roi*, the God who sees us (Genesis 16:13). But what I love more than knowing he sees us is knowing he cares about us and meets the needs he sees. Since God sees us and loves us in this way, this is the way we should see and love the people in our lives—our family, friends, acquaintances, and strangers alike. Let us not underestimate the value of something as "insignificant" as a look.

Make eye contact with the people around you. Remember purposeful eye contact communicates to people they are seen and valued. Letting them know you see them could help them realize God sees them too.

Prayer Prompt

Father, thank you for being the God who sees. Help me to keep my eyes fixed on you and to see other people as you do. Forgive me for the times I have been blinded to things and people you wanted me to see. Remind me to look each person in the eyes and help me to see their beautiful soul you created. Amen.

A Little Sacrifice

Therefore, I urge you, brothers and sisters, in view of God's mercy, to offer your bodies as a living sacrifice, holy and pleasing to God—this is your true and proper worship.

ROMANS 12:1

In the writing industry, the chance to pitch an idea to an agent or publisher is difficult to come by. So I was thrilled when I was able to attend a writer's conference where I was given the rare opportunity to pitch my book proposal to people in these positions. After my meetings, I joined the other writers for a time of fellowship in the lobby. As I was chatting with a new writer friend, she shocked me with an unbelievably generous offer.

"I have a publisher appointment tomorrow, and I feel like God is telling me to give it to you," Micah said.

I reluctantly yet respectfully declined. "I could never take your appointment. It's yours."

Then, with even more conviction, she responded, "It's meant to be yours, and if I don't give it to you, I would be in disobedience to the Lord."

Who can argue with that, right? So before we parted ways for the evening, I thanked her and told her I'd pray about it. The next morning, I woke up to a text with a picture of the meeting schedule with Micah's name marked out and my name written in her place.

I couldn't believe my eyes. How could someone love another person, especially a stranger, so sacrificially?

Jesus taught the value of this kind of sacrificial love when he said, "My command is this: Love each other as I have loved you. Greater love has no one than this: to lay down one's life for one's friends" (John 15:12–13).

While Jesus doesn't intend for us to die for our friends in a literal sense, he does intend for us to lay aside our own selfish desires and put the needs of others first. This may mean sacrificing your sleep, resources, tastebuds, comfort, wish list, hobbies, timeline, likes, recognition, rewards, or other things you might find hard to give up.

The key is learning to value others' interests more than our own. This is what Micah modeled for me. Such love reminds me of our Savior, who not only taught the concept but also demonstrated it.

In the ultimate act of sacrificial love, Jesus gave his life for us. On the cross, he took our place and marked out our transgressions so our names could be forever written in his book. Because he loved us sacrificially, we now are to love others in the same way. While this feels impossible to do on our own, it is possible because we have his Holy Spirit living in us. With his empowerment, we can act in ways contrary to our fleshly nature.

I pray we follow his lead and surrender our will as he and Micah so beautifully displayed. Let's not lose sight of the eternal impact our sacrifice can have. Jesus sacrificed so we could be with him for all of eternity. Could our sacrifice lead others to join him in eternity as well?

Your Little Task

How can you sacrificially love someone in your own life today?
Write down the name of someone you can serve and schedule a
time to make it happen. Pray for the strength and discipline to act
selflessly and sacrificially toward that person.

Prayer Prompt

*Lord, thank you for your never-ending love. May
I never forget the magnitude of your sacrifice on
the cross for me. Fill me with your love so I may
love those around me as you have loved me. Help
me to lay down my own selfish desires and notice
the needs of others. Enable me to sacrificially show
them your love with all I am. Amen.*

A Little Forgiveness

Bear with each other and forgive one another if any of you has a grievance against someone. Forgive as the Lord forgave you.

COLOSSIANS 3:13

On the drive to school one rainy, hurried morning, I snapped at my daughter Kate over something minuscule. As soon as the words exited my mouth, I regretted them. Evidenced by the tears in her eyes and the deafening silence, I knew I had messed up. So, when I pulled into the parking lot, I offered an olive branch prayer over the two of us. With a slight smirk and squeeze of my hand, she left for school.

All day, I couldn't shake the feeling that I had failed as her mother. Three o'clock couldn't come soon enough; I wanted to apologize again and make it right. In an effort to redeem myself, I bought a new journal for the two of us to share. I wrote our names and the year at the top of the first blank page, followed by the simple words, "I'm sorry. Please forgive me."

At the end of her school day, I watched her tentatively walk to the car, unsure of what kind of atmosphere she would be entering. I handed her the journal and silently waited for her response. As she read those five little words, more tears filled her eyes—this time, however, they were glistening with forgiveness and love.

While this specific story ended happily and quickly, I know many of our stories do not. Let's face it, choosing forgiveness can be one of the most difficult decisions we make.

It is especially hard when the person who hurt us has done so repeatedly, and it's even harder when they aren't repentant. Forgiveness is a process. Just when we think we've made progress, something triggers the old wound, and we have to forgive all over again.

As believers, we are called to forgive without limit. When asked how many times we should forgive, Jesus responded, "Seventy times seven!" (Matthew 18:22 NLT). In essence, he was saying we shouldn't keep track of how many times we forgive someone.

Jesus not only taught on this subject but also demonstrated it. He forgave those who repented as well as those he hoped would eventually repent. From the woman caught in adultery (John 8:3–11), to Peter denying he knew Jesus (John 18:15–18, 25–27; 21:15–19), to the criminal on the cross (Luke 23:39–43), and even to the people who crucified him (Luke 23:34). There was no limit to his forgiveness, no matter the severity of the pain and rejection he endured.

Friend, this was true then and it is still true now. The Bible tells us God has cast our sins as far as the east is from the west (Psalm 103:11–12) and that he remembers our sins no more (Hebrews 8:12). Since Jesus loved us enough to forgive us, may we follow his example by lovingly offering forgiveness to those who hurt us. The key is to remember how much he has forgiven us. He died on the cross for our past, present, and future sins. If he could do that much for us, forgiving others is the least we can do.

Reflect on how completely God has forgiven you. Once you realize the magnitude of the forgiveness he has offered you, consider who in your life you need to forgive. Offer your forgiveness to them verbally, if appropriate, as well as inwardly in your heart.

Lord, thank you for forgiving me of all of my sins. Please help me accept your forgiveness, forgive myself, and forgive those in my life who have hurt me. Produce in me a generous attitude of forgiveness toward others so we can share in your freedom. Show me if there's someone in my life whom I have hurt and give me the strength to humbly ask them for their forgiveness. Amen.

A Little Cup

Then he took the cup, and when he had given thanks, he gave it to them, and they all drank from it. "This is my blood of the covenant, which is poured out for many," he said to them.

MARK 14:23–24

I hadn't had a girls' trip away since having my children, so when I had the opportunity to travel to a mountain retreat with a group of women from MOPS (Mothers of Preschoolers), I was grateful. I couldn't wait to stay up late, eat what I wanted, and talk with my friends so I could return to my family rejuvenated and ready to serve them again.

With no midnight cries to disrupt my slumber, I woke up early to the sunrise peeking over the mountains. Slippers on my feet and Bible in hand, I nestled comfortably into the wooden rocker on the porch, ready for some much-needed quiet time with the Lord.

Most of the other moms were taking advantage of the same beautiful view and quiet. So I was surprised when one of the MOPS mentors approached me with a coffee pot and a mug. "Would you like a cup?" Mrs. Betty offered with a smile.

Mind you, she was also at the cabin for a relaxing getaway. I'm sure Mrs. Betty would have loved to be served, yet she chose to serve us younger mothers. As I think back upon Mrs. Betty, I realize it wasn't anything she necessarily said that has stuck with me. Instead, it was the humility and heart behind her actions that have left their mark.

At the last supper, Jesus also offered a cup. After giving thanks for the bread and breaking it, he said, "Take it; this is my body." Then he took the cup, gave thanks, and offered it to the disciples, and they all drank from it. As they drank, he said, "This is my blood of the covenant, which is poured out for many" (Mark 14:22–24). This little cup symbolized so much. It foreshadowed his crucifixion and ultimate offering of himself.

Only a few verses later, Jesus agonized in the garden before his death. Praying to the Father, he said, "Take this cup from me. Yet not what I will, but what you will" (Mark 14:36). God the Father didn't take the cup from his Son because Jesus "did not come to be served, but to serve, and give his life as a ransom for many" (Matthew 20:28). The humility and heart behind our Savior's act of love have undoubtedly left their mark too—for all of eternity.

Imagine sitting at the last supper with Jesus as he offers you a cup. Unlike the disciples, we have a better understanding of Jesus' overture. Will you accept his offer? The same offer is still extended to us today. May we daily take his cup in remembrance of all he has done for us. It is only when we allow him to fill our cups that we are able to fill the cups of those who are feeling empty around us. So today, this is me offering what I have in my cup to you. Whose cup is God leading you to fill?

Your Little Task

Offer a cup of coffee, tea, or lemonade to those God reveals to you who might be in need of refreshment. Pray it opens the door not just for physical refreshment but for emotional and spiritual refreshment as well.

Prayer Prompt

Father, thank you for the blood of the new covenant you poured out for me. May I never forget the love you have offered me. I know my cup is empty without you. Fill me, Lord, so I may pour your love out to everyone around me. Amen.

A Little Number

For God so loved the world that he gave his one and only Son,
that whoever believes in him shall not perish but have eternal life.

JOHN 3:16

My son, Will, loves sports. His first word was *ball*, and he's always
had one in his hands. When he was a toddler, he loved it when I
chased him around the house and when I made obstacle courses
for him to run through. When he would act stubbornly and refuse
to get dressed, eat his peas, or whatever other task he considered
burdensome, we would tell him it was a race. He was so competitive that he would scarf down all his peas and dress in something
other than pajamas whether he liked them or not!

This competitive nature has remained with Will as he has
grown into adolescence. As he moves from sport to sport with the
changing seasons, he calls each sport his favorite. Regardless of
what sport Will is playing or what number is on his jersey, I scour
the fields and courts to find him through the crowds of players.
On the occasions I can't locate him, my heart is unsettled until
I do. So I try to keep my eyes on him because he is my favorite
player. He is always my number one. My heart swells as I watch
him do what he loves.

As his daughter, God loves watching you too. Do you realize
he is your number one fan? Throughout his Word, we see how much
he values every person. In the Gospel of Luke, Jesus told three parables to reinforce his love for the individual. The first was the parable
of the lost sheep. Jesus said, "Suppose one of you has a hundred

sheep and loses one of them. Doesn't he leave the ninety-nine in the open country and go after the lost sheep until he finds it? And when he finds it, he joyfully puts it on his shoulders and goes home. Then he calls his friends and neighbors together and says, 'Rejoice with me; I have found my lost sheep'" (Luke 15:4–7).

Jesus continues his point with the parable of the lost coin. He said, "Suppose a woman has ten silver coins and loses one. Doesn't she light a lamp, sweep the house and search carefully until she finds it? And when she does find it?...She calls her friends and neighbors together and says, 'Rejoice with me; I have found my lost coin'" (Luke 15:8–10).

To drive his point home, Jesus finished with the parable of the lost son. He told a story about a man who had two sons. The younger one squandered his wealth with wild living. After he had spent everything and reached his lowest point, he returned home. His father brought the best robe, a ring, and sandals for his feet. They had a feast and celebrated the son who was lost but who was now found (Luke 15:11–32).

In each of these parables, the sheep, the coin, and the son represent us. God's love for the individual is so great that he seeks each one and rejoices when they are found. He sought after you, and now he seeks after those who are still lost and then joyfully forgives them. This is the kind of love that prompted Jesus to come to the earth to search for lost people and save them. This is the extraordinary love that caused God to give "his one and only Son" (John 3:16).

When I think about how much I love my son, I cannot fathom ever having to give him up. But that is the sacrifice God made so that no one would remain lost for eternity, and that is the sacrifice Jesus made on the cross. While bigger numbers and more influence threaten to steal our focus, God is reminding us to focus on the one—him and the ones he loves.

Your Little Task

Ask God to show you who in your life might be lost. Look for opportunities to share God's love and affirm their individual value to him.

Prayer Prompt

Lord, thank you for giving your one and only
Son for me. I am so grateful for his love for me
displayed by his sacrifice on the cross. Forgive me
for focusing on the masses and help me to focus
on whomever it is you want me to see. May I be as
concerned about seeking and saving the ones who
are lost as you are. Amen.

DAY 49

A Little Object

Then the Lord said to him,
"What is that in your hand?"

EXODUS 4:2

A friend of mine bakes cookies for an antitrafficking ministry. After being packaged in bags containing a handwritten note of encouragement and an emergency phone number the recipient can call for help, the cookies are distributed to women who are at risk of—or already are—being trafficked. As the volunteers offer the sweet treat, they also offer to pray for the women they meet.

While talking about this project, my friend Linda commented that she is amazed at how making cookies—and making a mess in her kitchen—has become her ministry. By simply giving of her time and using the everyday utensils and appliances in front of her, she makes an impact in her community. I wonder how many women have been blessed and how many lives have been transformed by the spatula in Linda's hand.[6]

God loves to use ordinary objects for his extraordinary purposes. We see this revealed in the Bible over and over again. One of my favorite examples is found in the story of Moses. When God told him to free the Israelites from the Egyptian pharaoh, Moses made excuses because he felt inadequate. God assured Moses he

---

6   Rachael Adams, "'The Love Offering Blog Series: Using What God Has Placed in Our Hands' by Linda Grim," Rachael Adams (website), December 10, 2020, https://rachaelkadams.com/the-love-offering-blog-series-using-what-god-has-placed-in-our-hands-by-linda-grim/.

would be with him, and then he asked Moses what was in his hand. This seems like a strange question to ask, but Moses' response was even more strange because Moses was holding a shepherd's staff. He wasn't holding a weapon or piece of armor like you'd think he would need when approaching Pharoah to demand the release of the Israelites. Rather, it was just a wooden rod with a curved hook at the top. Basically, it was a stick. Shepherds used these staffs for walking, guiding sheep, and killing snakes, among other things—not for going into battle. As simple as it was, God used this shepherd's staff to perform miraculous signs through Moses and to lead thousands to freedom (Exodus 4).

Other heroes of faith used ordinary objects to accomplish God-given missions too. Joshua used a trumpet to flatten the walls of Jericho (Joshua 6). Gideon used a fleece to confirm God's will (Judges 6). Samson used a donkey's jawbone to defeat one thousand Philistines (Judges 15). David used a small stone to kill Goliath (1 Samuel 17). Elijah used oil to demonstrate God's power to provide (2 Kings 4). Little did these men know the power their simple items would wield. Of course, these things in and of themselves don't have power. It is God who empowered the resources they used, but each man was obedient to use them.

While it is easy to assume God can use only special objects, let's not discount his use of the everyday items we have. What ordinary things has God placed in your hands—possibly a pen, paint brush, stethoscope, broom, hammer, ball, computer, or microphone? Whatever they may be, they can be instruments for him. The key is that they are dedicated for his use. Let the objects be reminders of his power and presence, realizing it really isn't about what is in our hands but the fact that God holds us in his.

Take inventory of what God has placed in your hands. Pray you steward well what he has given you.

Lord, thank you for giving me tools and resources. I don't want to take any object for granted. Help me to recognize what you have given me and show me how each item can be used for good. I dedicate everything I have for your service in order to further your kingdom. Amen.

A Little Vision

Where there is no vision, the people perish.
PROVERBS 29:18 KJV

I have trouble envisioning things. This is particularly true with home design and decor. I need to see a picture of something (thank you, Pinterest) or see it in person before I know whether I will like it. For example, when we were considering painting our yellow house white, I asked every friend I knew with a white house what shade of white they had selected. Once I saw their homes in person, I went to our local paint store and purchased samples. When I returned home, I painted six strips of vinyl, each with a different hue, and I took pictures at different times of day to account for the effect varying levels of light would have on each shade. Despite all this, I was still paralyzed by indecision. I just couldn't envision the finished product.

While envisioning is a struggle of mine, I also realize its importance. Especially in regard to more serious topics, not just when designing our homes. Without a vision, it is less likely we will realize our goals. If we don't know where we are going or whom we want to become, it's hard to know where to start and what steps to take. A vision helps us create a better plan and be more organized along the way. Solomon, one of the wisest men to live, said it this way: "Where there is no vision, the people perish" (Proverbs 29:18 KJV). His statement may sound dramatic, but without vision, we remain stagnant and paralyzed by inactivity.

This certainly wasn't the case for Nehemiah. While serving as a cupbearer for a Persian king, Nehemiah learned that the walls and gates of Jerusalem were in disrepair. He was burdened for the Jews living there, who were left defenseless and vulnerable to attack. God put a desire in Nehemiah's heart to rebuild the walls and gave him a vision for the work. As Nehemiah talked to God, a plan began to form in his mind, and his role in rebuilding the city walls became clear.

Despite resistance, Nehemiah continued building the wall that, according to historians, was around twenty-five feet high, twenty-two feet wide, and 2.5 miles long—and he finished this project in just fifty-two days![7] See what God can do in just fifty-two days!

The people thought it couldn't be done. The job was too big, and the problems were too great. But with God's help, they accomplished a seemingly impossible task. The Bible records that enemies and friends alike recognized that the Israelites' success could only be attributed to God, which in turn led to a religious revival for the city (Nehemiah 6:15–16).

If what Solomon said about lack of vision causing people to perish is true, then the reverse should also be accurate. With vision, people will survive and hopefully thrive. While we may struggle to envision what the finished product should be, God has a perfect design. And friend, he is building something beautiful.

Your Little Task

Is there a project that excites you in your community? Join in the work and help finish the project to see the vision come to fruition.

---

7   "History of Jerusalem's Walls & Gates," Holy Land Site (website), accessed September 9, 2021, https://www.holylandsite.com/walls-of-jerusalem-history.

Lord, help me to see the world from your perspective. Give me a vision to help others and an action plan to see the vision fulfilled. Surround me with people whom I can inspire with the vision, and let us work as a team to accomplish your goals. Show me how to join with those to whom you have already revealed a portion of your plan. Unite us, Lord, to see your kingdom come and your will be done, on earth as it is in heaven. Amen.

A Little Less

For it is by grace you have been saved, through faith—
and this is not from yourselves, it is the gift of God—
not by works, so that no one can boast.

EPHESIANS 2:8–9

As an achiever and perfectionist by nature, I have a tendency to always want to do more and be better. In fact, my family jokes that I am a gold star girl. Growing up, I was motivated by a chore chart where I would place gold star stickers beside completed tasks. I wish I could tell you I no longer have this tendency, but even in adulthood, I still love a good list where I can put a line through the tasks I have accomplished. I've even been known to add something to the list that I have already accomplished so I have the gratification of crossing it out too!

The root of this tendency to achieve and strive is unclear, but I know there is nothing I can do to make God love me any more than he does, and there is nothing I can do to make him love me any less.[8] However, our culture communicates quite the opposite. In today's culture there is constant pressure to do more and be better, but what if God's answer is to actually do less?

Let's take a look at Naaman's story found in 2 Kings. Naaman was commander of the army of the king of Aram. He was a courageous soldier afflicted with leprosy. A young girl who served Naaman's wife said to her mistress, "If only my master

---

[8] J. D. Greear, "The Gospel Prayer," J. D. Greear Ministries (website), last modified August 27, 2016, https://jdgreear.com/the-gospel-prayer/.

would see the prophet who is in Samaria! He would cure him of his leprosy" (5:1–3).

Searching for a cure, Naaman first went to the king of Israel for healing, but the king denied his request. The prophet Elisha heard of Naaman's predicament and offered to help. Elisha instructed Naaman to wash himself seven times in the Jordan River and promised his flesh would be restored and he would be cleansed (vv. 4–10). The story continues:

> But Naaman went away angry and said, "I thought that he would surely come out to me and stand and call on the name of the LORD his God, wave his hand over the spot and cure me of my leprosy. Are not Abana and Pharpar, the rivers of Damascus, better than all the waters of Israel? Couldn't I wash in them and be cleansed?" So he turned and went off in a rage. Naaman's servants went to him and said, "My father, if the prophet had told you to do some great thing, would you not have done it? How much more, then, when he tells you, 'Wash and be cleansed'!" (vv. 11–13)

Naaman finally did as Elisha had advised, and his flesh was restored and cleansed. Then Naman went back to Elisha to thank him and give his life to the Lord (vv. 14–26).

In this account, the young girl who served Naaman's wife inspires me. We don't know her name or much about her, but her brief suggestion to her mistress brought healing and faith in God to a powerful Aramaean commander. God placed her for a purpose, and she was faithful. Through her we learn what to do, and through Naaman we learn what not to do.

Since Naaman was a great hero, he was used to getting respect and royal treatment, which might explain why he was outraged when Elisha treated him like an ordinary person. To wash in a great river would be one thing, but the Jordan River was small and dirty. Naaman thought washing in the Jordan River was beneath a man of his position. He left in a rage because the cure for his disease seemed too simple. Full of pride, Naaman could not accept the simple cure of faith.

While we like to think of ourselves differently, how often do we react to God's offer of grace in the same way? Just to believe in Jesus somehow doesn't seem significant enough to warrant eternal life. What Naaman had to do to wash his leprosy away is similar to what we must do to have our sins washed away—humbly accept God's mercy. It is by faith we are saved, not by works, so no one can boast (Ephesians 2:8–9). While productivity can be a good thing, sometimes the answer might be doing less so God can do more.

Your Little Task

No matter how small your position or task, humbly obey God's directives and watch the healing and cleansing that can take place for you and others around you.

Prayer Prompt

Lord, thank you for your work on the cross.
Remind me that it is finished. Forgive me for
striving and falsely believing I must do better to
receive your best. Help me to humbly obey you in
faith no matter how simple it may seem to me.
Amen.

A Little by Little

The LORD your God will drive out those nations before you,
little by little. You will not be allowed to eliminate them all at once,
or the wild animals will multiply around you.

DEUTERONOMY 7:22

Do you ever get overwhelmed by the size of the task in front of you? I certainly do. When I began writing this devotional, I stared at the blank page and blinking cursor, thinking to myself, *How will I ever finish this?* When we moved houses, I stared at the boxes, tape, and the belongings we had accumulated, and I stood paralyzed, unsure where to begin. When we decided to build a home, we stared at the land before us, excited but overwhelmed by how much needed to be done before we could live there.

You've been there too, right? Whether it is your job, family responsibilities, or personal goals, I'm sure you can relate. However, in these moments we have a choice. We can stare at our seemingly insurmountable tasks and stay stuck, or we can stare at our Savior and start moving toward our goal, one step at a time. I don't always get this right. But, when I do, I'm amazed by what a difference a little movement can make.

With my writing, one letter turned into one word, which turned into one sentence, which turned into one paragraph. The paragraphs together made a page and then a devotion. Fifty-two devotions later, my manuscript was complete. The same was true of packing boxes when we moved. I packed a little each day, moving from room to room, and after a month, the movers arrived, and the house was empty. The same was true for the construction of our new home. Each day we could see the evidence of the contractor's work on our house. Within a year, we were staring at the same set of boxes, only this time we were unpacking them, again one room at a time.

While we wish we could snap our fingers or wave a magic wand to complete the tasks before us or solve our problems, life doesn't work that way. So often we feel the pressure to "build Rome in a day," but even God didn't create the world in a day. He created the universe little by little. He could have created everything he wanted to in a moment, but he chose to create it in six days and rest on the seventh (Genesis 1). Good things take time and happen little by little.

God's little-by-little approach applies not only to creation but also to how he often solves problems. Obviously, God has the power to fix anything instantly, but sometimes his answers come in small increments. In the book of Exodus, God told the Israelites he would destroy their enemies but not all at once. He said, "I will not drive them out in a single year, because the land would become desolate and the wild animals too numerous for you. Little by little I will drive them out before you, until you have increased enough to take possession of the land" (23:29–30).

Through these examples, we can see not all of God's solutions are instantaneous, but his purposeful delay does not justify our inaction. In the case of the Israelites, God's plan required constant cooperation and persistence. Their success toward the promised land occurred step by step.

God could miraculously and instantaneously change our lives. But as demonstrated in Scripture, it is evident he chooses to help gradually, teaching us one lesson at a time to sanctify and sharpen us. We can trust God to make up the difference between where we want to be and where we are now. And, when we look back on it all, we will see a miraculous transformation that transpired little by little.

Your Little Task

Look over your journey of little tasks. Reflect on how God has taken your little a long way.

Prayer Prompt

Lord, thank you for giving me examples in Scripture. When I feel overwhelmed by the tasks before me or the enormity of the problems surrounding me, show me the next small step. I trust that, little by little, I am being molded into who you want me to be. Help me be patient in the waiting and give me encouragement to carry on until my task is complete. Amen.

A Little Bit More

The purpose of this devotional is to help all of us see how small individual acts in our daily lives lead to a significant impact in the kingdom of God. The goal was to keep each daily task as simple and as burdenless as possible. This book isn't meant to create one more thing you need to add to your life so you can do more or be more.

However, if any of the devotions were particularly significant to you and you are questioning what more you could do to expand on a task, I wanted to give you a few more ideas. Again, this isn't a to-do list; rather, I pray it becomes a lifestyle where our inner beliefs are outwardly expressed. And of course, if you want to read through the devotions again, these could provide inspiration for rounds two, three, and ongoing.

- A Little Beginning—Spur someone on to begin, persevere, or to begin again.
- A Little Love—Demonstrate your love for God by loving others. Think of something you could do to show his love to someone in your life. Then do it!
- A Little Vessel—Display an empty vessel somewhere in your home as a reminder to allow God to fill you each day.
- A Little Invitation—Invite someone to join you at church.
- A Little Yes—Ask God to reveal an area where you need to say no. This will open space for a better yes.
- A Little Encounter—Reach out to someone to let them know how much an encounter with them has meant to you.
- A Little Presence—Think about who needs the gift of your presence. Show up and simply sit with them.

- A Little Group—Pray about starting a Bible study or fellowship group of your own.
- A Little Belief—In what area do you struggle to believe in yourself? Ask God to reveal a truth to you to help you believe in who he made you to be.
- A Little Preparation—Encourage another person who is in a season of preparation.
- A Little Meal—Take someone a meal.
- A Little Walk—Take a prayer walk around your community.
- A Little Dream—Write down your dream. Date it and tell a trusted friend about it.
- A Little Perspective—Ask God to reveal his perspective on your situation. Is there an area you have been looking at through an earthly lens that he wants you to see through an eternal lens?
- A Little Work—In order to bring meaning into your mundane, invite God into each activity throughout your day.
- A Little Song—Send a worship song to a friend.
- A Little Companionship—Visit a nursing home.
- A Little Celebration—Throw someone else a party.
- A Little Time—Purchase a watch or hourglass for yourself or someone else as a reminder of the value of time.
- A Little Touch—Offer a tender touch to someone the world considers untouchable.
- A Little Prayer—Write down the prayer requests of friends and family members, intercede continually for them, and then record when and how God answers.

- A Little Faith—Faith is confidence in what we hope for and assurance about what we do not see. Take a step of faith toward something you hope for but don't yet see.
- A Little Conversation—Make a list of conversation starters. Use an idea from your list to start a conversation with the next person you come into contact with.
- A Little Money—Give a donation to a charity of your choice.
- A Little Effort—Is there an area where you have become lackadaisical or stopped putting forth effort? Pray that God would help you make an extra effort on behalf of others.
- A Little Humility—Jesus came to serve rather than to be served. How can you humble yourself and serve someone else?
- A Little Hospitality—Do one thing to practice hospitality.
- A Little Grace—Give yourself grace today.
- A Little Inclusion—Is there someone you have excluded in the past? Include them in your group or at your next social gathering.
- A Little Testimony—Write down your testimony and be ready to share it with someone.
- A Little Tradition—Think about what God has done for you. Is there a way you can start a new tradition to honor him?
- A Little Gesture—How can you act selflessly today? Offer to help someone in need.

- A Little Letter—Write an encouraging note and leave it in a place where a stranger could find it.
- A Little Courage—Is there something wrong in the world that you wish you could change but you feel frustrated by the sense that there is little you can do about it? Today, face your fear and take one courageous step toward righting that wrong. Trust God to use your effort, no matter how small it seems.
- A Little Thought—Tell someone you are thinking of them and that they are amazing!
- A Little Clothing—If you are crafty or a seamstress, consider making clothing or knitting a scarf to give away.
- A Little Gratitude—Gratitude is more than just saying thank you; it is a posture of your heart. Look for small things that you count as blessings each day to thank God for. If you haven't already, start a gratitude journal.
- A Little Encouragement—See how many people you can encourage today!
- A Little Story—Share a Bible verse with another person in your life. Consider purchasing a Bible or a devotional for them.
- A Little Interruption—Instead of holding back out of fear that you are interrupting someone, politely interject yourself into a situation or conversation. Who knows where it may lead?
- A Little Perseverance—Is there someone you know who is on the verge of giving up too soon? Encourage them to persevere.
- A Little Seed—If it is planting season, plant a seed and watch it grow. Give away the fruit, vegetable, or flower

that your seed produces. Alternatively, purchase a packet of seeds or bulbs and attach a card with Matthew 13:31–32 written on it. Then, give it to someone as a reminder that even their smallest acts of love and service are significant.

- A Little Kindness—Reflect on how God and others have been kind to you and reciprocate their kindness.
- A Little Look—Make a conscious effort to look less at your technological devices and look more into the eyes of the people around you.
- A Little Sacrifice—Who has sacrificed greatly for you? Thank them. If no one comes to mind, thank someone in the military for their sacrifice and service.
- A Little Forgiveness—As hard as it is to admit, sometimes we cause pain and are the ones who need to ask for forgiveness. And sometimes we even have to forgive ourselves. Consider whether you need to extend forgiveness to yourself or ask someone else for their forgiveness.
- A Little Cup—Purchase a cup with a cute saying or Scripture on it to give away to the person God lays on your heart.
- A Little Number—Have bigger numbers stolen your focus? Focus on the one individual in front of you.
- A Little Object—Praise someone for the work they do with the object God has placed in their hands.
- A Little Vision—Ask God to give you a clear vision for how to meet a need in your community. Share the vision with a confidant and pray God gives you the appropriate

action steps and surrounds you with a group of people to help you accomplish the goal.

- A Little Less—Where have you been exhausting yourself? Rest. Be still and know that God is with you (Psalm 46:10).
- A Little by Little—What is the next little step you need to take to eventually complete a big task or solve a big problem? Try to make a little progress toward that goal today.

If you are really feeling motivated after reading the entire devotional, your final little task is to give it away, let someone borrow it, or purchase one for a friend. Ten percent of all proceeds from the sale of this book will be given to charity. Your little purchase of this devotional will go a long way in the hearts and lives of others. Thank you!

A Little List of Tasks

☐ **A Little Beginning**

What is God asking you to begin or begin again? Start a record of the small steps you are taking toward your goal. Celebrate your progress and growth. Make note of each new milestone, but remember that much of your growth will be on the inside.

☐ **A Little Love**

Settle in your heart that God is your first love and open your heart to receive his love. Without his love you have nothing of significance to give.

☐ **A Little Vessel**

Turn your hands with your palms facing up to God. In this posture, pray God would fill your empty vessel and commit to him that you will pour out to what he's given you to fill others too.

☐ **A Little Invitation**

Knowing how God can use a little invitation to make a significant impact, think about to whom you can extend an invitation. Who knows where it may lead?

☐ **A Little Yes**

If you have said yes to God as your Lord and Savior, ask him to reveal your next step of obedience. Then say yes.

☐ **A Little Encounter**

View the next encounter you have with a person as one that has the potential to change everything! Consider how an encounter with you could lead to the other person having an encounter with Christ.

☐ A Little Presence
It's possible to be present in the body but not present in mind and heart. When you are with others, make sure you give them your full attention.

☐ A Little Group
Consider joining a small group through your church. Watch how God uses the group of believers to further his kingdom for his glory.

☐ A Little Belief
Think about someone in your life who might be struggling to believe in Christ, believe in themselves, or both. How can you come alongside to encourage them to believe?

☐ A Little Preparation
Reflect on how God has prepared you for your current season. What can you do to better prepare for the season ahead?

☐ A Little Meal
What is your favorite meal? Invite someone to share it with you.

☐ A Little Walk
Take a walk and pay attention to the people you pass. Ask God to give you the opportunity to be a good Samaritan.

☐ A Little Dream
After praying and spending time with God, finish this sentence: "I have a dream to…"

☐ A Little Perspective
Offer someone your outside perspective. They may be struggling to recognize how much they are accomplishing or to see God's

presence in their present situation. Help them to see themselves the way God sees them.

☐ A Little Work
Ask God to reveal the kingdom impact of your daily jobs and chores. No matter what work you do, pray God helps you realize your significant contribution.

☐ A Little Song
Make intentional choices to turn on worship music today. Sing along in praise to the Lord.

☐ A Little Companionship
Do you know someone who might be lonely and in need of companionship? Go and simply spend time with them.

☐ A Little Celebration
When you hear someone sharing good news, do you react with jealousy or celebration? Be intentional about celebrating others even for small victories. Watch how they react as you cheer them on.

☐ A Little Time
Ask God to reveal the value of the moments in your life. Make space to intentionally focus on these moments and cherish each one.

☐ A Little Touch
Offer a handshake, pat on the back, hug, or a hand to hold. Don't be surprised if the person you reach out to responds with, "I needed that!"

☐ A Little Prayer
Think of someone in your life who needs prayer. Bow your head and pray.

☐ A Little Faith
Read Hebrews 11 and think about what the heroes of faith were commended for. Finish this sentence: "By faith (your name)…"

☐ A Little Conversation
Smile and say hello to the next person you pass. If someone speaks to you, engage with them and continue the conversation.

☐ A Little Money
Spend money on someone else today. Let the Lord lead you on whom to bless.

☐ A Little Effort
Ask God to open your spiritual eyes to see the need of others. Be intentional to prioritize meeting those needs.

☐ A Little Humility
Reflect on the gifts God has given you. Give him all the glory for any success or accomplishment in your life.

☐ A Little Hospitality
Whom do you feel God is leading you to host in your home? How can you prepare and be present with that person?

☐ A Little Grace
Thank God for his undeserved favor. Ask him to reveal if you have been judgmental and if there is someone in your life to whom you need to extend grace. Settle that in your heart today and, if you need to, tell the other person.

☐ A Little Inclusion
Think about whether you have a tendency to exclude others. Then, the next time you are in a social environment, take notice of your

surroundings and look for ways to include someone who may feel left out.

☐ A Little Testimony
Reflect on your testimony to see how God has been present in your life.

☐ A Little Tradition
What is your favorite tradition? Be intentional about connecting to God and others as you commemorate these special occasions.

☐ A Little Gesture
Set aside an umbrella. The next time it's raining and you see someone without an umbrella, give them yours.

☐ A Little Letter
Write a letter to someone whom God places on your heart. Prayerfully consider what God might have you say to them.

☐ A Little Courage
Next time you are faced with a fear, reach out for the hand of the Lord and let him guide you forward in faith.

☐ A Little Thought
Pay attention to your thoughts. Catch any negative thought and replace it with a truth from Scripture.

☐ A Little Clothing
Look for opportunities to share your clothing with others by donating or simply letting them borrow something for an occasion.

☐ A Little Gratitude

When someone does something for you or says something kind, say thank you. Perhaps it's even the Lord you need to thank.

☐ A Little Encouragement

Make a list of your favorite encouraging phrases. Feel free to look at the examples I offered. Then, share your encouragement with someone whom God places on your heart.

☐ A Little Story

Share a story from the Bible with someone else. Talk about how God is speaking to you through the Scriptures.

☐ A Little Interruption

How do you see people who interrupt your schedule? As annoyances or as the reason for your life and ministry? The next time you are interrupted, take the time to stop and give the person your full attention. It very well could be a divine interruption.

☐ A Little Perseverance

Get quiet with the Lord and ask him to reveal any areas or relationships you gave up on too soon. Resolve to begin again and finish what you started.

☐ A Little Seed

Plant a seed and watch it grow as a daily reminder of God's work in you.

☐ A Little Kindness

Look around to see how you might be able to show kindness to others. Choose one little act of kindness that would be significant to someone God puts on your heart.

☐ A Little Look

Make eye contact with the people around you. Remember purposeful eye contact communicates to people that they are seen and valued. Letting them know you see them could help them realize God sees them too.

☐ A Little Sacrifice

How can you sacrificially love someone in your own life today? Write down the name of someone you can serve and schedule a time to make it happen. Pray for the strength and discipline to act selflessly and sacrificially toward that person.

☐ A Little Forgiveness

Reflect on how completely God has forgiven you. Once you realize the magnitude of the forgiveness he has offered you, consider who in your life you need to forgive. Offer your forgiveness to them verbally, if appropriate, as well as inwardly in your heart.

☐ A Little Cup

Offer a cup of coffee, tea, or lemonade to those God reveals to you who might be in need of refreshment. Pray it opens the door not just for physical refreshment but for emotional and spiritual refreshment as well.

☐ A Little Number

Ask God to show you who in your life might be lost. Look for opportunities to share God's love and affirm their individual value to him.

☐ A Little Object

Take inventory of what God has placed in your hands. Pray you steward well what he has given you.

☐ A Little Vision

Is there a project that excites you in your community? Join in the work and help finish the project to see the vision come to fruition.

☐ A Little Less

No matter how small your position or task, humbly obey God's directives and watch the healing and cleansing that can take place for you and others around you.

☐ A Little by Little

Look over your journey of little tasks. Reflect on how God has taken your little a long way.

☐ A Little…

Complete a task God lays on your heart.

A Little Encouragement:

A Collection of Small Significant Reminders

Welcome

- People like you and me can accomplish great things in our everyday moments by offering all we are and all we have to God.
- We are making an eternal impact even when we don't see tangible results.

A Little Beginning

- God is the one who turns our ordinary lives into something extraordinary.
- God rejoices in what is right, not necessarily what is big.
- Be faithful in the small.
- Begin where you are, do what you can, and leave the results up to God.

A Little Love

- Without God's love, you have nothing of significance to give.
- Take me back to the basics.

A Little Vessel

· When we offer all we have, no matter how small and inadequate it may seem, we can trust God to turn it into immeasurably more than we can ask or imagine.

A Little Invitation

· Jesus calls us to come.

A Little Yes

· Watch what a willing heart and a lifetime of yeses can do.

A Little Encounter

· I can encounter God personally each day, not just in eternity.
· An encounter with Jesus changes everything.

A Little Presence

· Presence can be our ministry because he is present in us.
· All we have to do is show up—no special skill or talent required.

A Little Group

· It is not about the size of the group God has given you; rather, it is the magnitude of the One within you.

A Little Belief

· Our belief in God and his presence in us changes our belief in ourselves.

A Little Preparation

· Our whole lives are God's training ground.

A Little Meal

· Whether it's simple or extravagant, a meal can go a long way toward growing the bonds of love between family and friends.

A Little Walk

· If we see a neighbor with a need, whether physical, financial, emotional, or spiritual, being loving means acting to meet that need.

A Little Dream

· When we dream, we should consider: If this became a reality, would it please God?

A Little Perspective

· We can keep working and trust we are further along than our vantage point allows us to see.

A Little Work

· God makes our work meaningful when we devote it to him.

A Little Song

· Put a new song in my heart and on my lips so others may sing of your praises too.

A Little Companionship

· The Lord is ever-present and the best companion of all.

A Little Celebration

· We are all on God's team with the same end goal in mind. And spoiler alert, we are on the winning team!

A Little Time

· Realizing our days are numbered helps us to steward the little time we have wisely and for eternal good.

A Little Touch

· Your simple, wordless gestures could be exactly what is needed to strengthen a connection, soothe an emotion, communicate without a word, or heal a hurting heart.

A Little Prayer

· God never fails to follow through.

A Little Faith

· Be faithful in the doing.

A Little Conversation

· Though it is small and simple, there is immense power in our tongue.
· One little word can make all the difference.

A Little Money

· Any amount spent from the heart can yield an eternal dividend.
· I am a steward not an owner of the resources I have been given.

A Little Effort

· Allow human need to compel us to compassionate action.

A Little Humility

· When we truly understand who Christ is, our self-importance melts away. This is true humility, the basis for greatness in any work we do for the Lord.

A Little Hospitality

· It's okay to be both a Martha and a Mary.

A Little Grace

· We can give grace freely because it was freely given to us.

A Little Inclusion

· We find our belonging in Jesus, knowing we are a part of his family.

A Little Testimony

· Come and see, then go and tell.

- We share what we love, and what could transform someone's life more than a relationship with God?

A Little Tradition

- The true heart of these traditions is connection to God and those around us.

A Little Gesture

- Small gestures can have lasting effects.
- Make a habit of sitting at Jesus' feet.

A Little Letter

- May our lives prove God is the author and that he alone holds the pen.

A Little Courage

- Fear can stop us from experiencing joy and realizing God-given plans.

A Little Thought

- We have to deliberately fill our minds with positive thoughts because what we consume becomes our inner narrative.

A Little Clothing

- Clothe me with a heart of compassion and kindness.

A Little Gratitude

- It isn't about reciprocity from people; it is about our reverence for God.

A Little Encouragement

- A little word of encouragement offered at the right moment can be the difference between finishing well and collapsing along the way.

A Little Story

- The important thing is that the story continues to be retold and explained—especially when that story is God's.

A Little Interruption

- The next interruption is likely an opportunity to be a part of his eternal plan.

A Little Perseverance

- I wonder how many times in our lives we would have realized our dream, the desire of our hearts, or the call on our lives if we had pushed through just a little longer.

A Little Seed

- Continue liberally sowing seeds no matter how small they seem and trust God to help them grow.

A Little Kindness

· We need the kindness of others all of the time, but we especially need it in the trying times.

A Little Look

· As we keep our eyes fixed on the Lord, we can take great comfort in knowing his eyes are also fixed on us.

A Little Sacrifice

· Let's not lose sight of the eternal impact our sacrifice can have.

A Little Forgiveness

· Forgiveness is a process.

A Little Cup

· It is only when we allow God to fill our cups that we are able to fill the cups of those around us who are feeling empty.

A Little Number

· God is reminding us to focus on the One.

A Little Object

· It really isn't about what is in our hands but the fact that God holds us in his.

A Little Vision

· See what God can do in just fifty-two days!

A Little Less

· While productivity can be a good thing, sometimes the answer might be doing less so God can do more.

A Little by Little

· We can trust God to make up the difference between where we want to be and where we are now.

A Little Inspiration:
Key Scriptures List

· A Little Beginning—"Do not despise small beginnings for the Lord rejoices to see the work begin" (Zechariah 4:10 NLT).

· A Little Love—"My command is this: Love each other as I have loved you" (John 15:12).

· A Little Vessel—"'Your servant has nothing there at all,' she said, 'except a small jar of olive oil'" (2 Kings 4:2).

· A Little Invitation—"Come, you who are blessed by my Father; take your inheritance, the kingdom prepared for you since the creation of the world" (Matthew 25:34).

· A Little Yes—"'I am the Lord's servant,' Mary answered. 'May it be as you have said'" (Luke 1:38).

· A Little Encounter—"Now he had to go through Samaria…Jesus, tired as he was from the journey, sat down by the well. It was about the sixth hour" (John 4:4–6).

· A Little Presence—"Never will I leave you; never will I forsake you" (Hebrews 13:5).

· A Little Group—"The Lord did not set his affection on you and choose you because you were more numerous than other peoples, for you were the fewest of all peoples" (Deuteronomy 7:7).

· A Little Belief—"Everything is possible for one who believes" (Mark 9:23).

· A Little Preparation—"My Father's house has many rooms; if that were not so, would I have told you that I am going there to prepare a place for you? And if I go and prepare a place for you, I will come back and take you to be with me that you also may be where I am" (John 14:2, 3).

· A Little Meal—"They devoted themselves to the apostles' teaching and to the fellowship, to the breaking of bread, and to prayer" (Acts 2:42).

· A Little Walk—"But a Samaritan, as he traveled, came where the man was; and when he saw him, he took pity on him" (Luke 10:33).

· A Little Dream—"When there is a prophet among you, I, the LORD, reveal myself to them in visions, I speak to them in dreams" (Numbers 12:6).

· A Little Perspective—"And Elisha prayed, 'Open his eyes, Lord, so that he may see.' Then the Lord opened the servant's eyes, and he looked and saw the hills full of horses and chariots of fire all around Elisha" (2 Kings 6:17).

· A Little Work—"Whatever you do, work at it with your whole heart, as working for the Lord, not for human masters, since you know that you will receive an inheritance from the Lord as a reward. It is the Lord Christ you are serving" (Colossians 3:23–24).

- A Little Song—"Sing to the LORD a new song; sing to the LORD, all the earth" (Psalm 96:1).

- A Little Companionship—"Ruth replied, 'Don't urge me to leave you or to turn back from you. Where you go I will go, and where you stay I will stay. Your people will be my people and your God will be my God'" (Ruth 1:16).

- A Little Celebration—"In a loud voice, she exclaimed: 'Blessed are you among women, and blessed is the child you will bear! But why am I so favored, that the mother of my Lord should come to me?'" (Luke 1:42–43).

- A Little Time—"What is your life? You are a mist that appears for a little while and then vanishes" (James 4:14).

- A Little Touch—"A man with leprosy came and knelt in front of Jesus, begging to be healed. 'If you are willing, you can heal me and make me clean,' he said. Moved with compassion, Jesus reached out and touched him. 'I am willing,' he said. 'Be healed!'" (Mark 1:40–41).

- A Little Prayer—"In the same way, the Spirit helps us in our weakness. We do not know what we ought to pray for, but the Spirit himself intercedes for us through wordless groans. And he who searches our hearts knows the mind of the Spirit because the Spirit intercedes

for God's people in accordance with the will of God"
(Romans 8:26–27).

- A Little Faith—"Without faith it is impossible to please
  God" (Hebrews 11:6).

- A Little Conversation—"The tongue has the power of
  life and death" (Proverbs 18:21).

- A Little Money—"Truly I tell you, this poor widow has
  put more into the treasury than all the others. They all
  gave out of their wealth; but she, out of her poverty, put
  in everything—all she had to live on" (Mark 12:43–44;
  cf. Luke 21:1–4).

- A Little Effort—"Some men came, bringing to him
  a paralyzed man, carried by four of them. Since they
  could not get him to Jesus because of the crowd, they
  made an opening in the roof above Jesus by digging
  through it and then lowered the mat the man was lying
  on" (Mark 2:3–4).

- A Little Humility—"Pride goes before destruction, a
  haughty spirit before a fall" (Proverbs 16:18).

- A Little Hospitality—"As Jesus and his disciples were on
  their way, he came to a village where a woman named
  Martha opened her home to him. She had a sister called
  Mary, who sat at the Lord's feet listening to what he
  said" (Luke 10:38–39).

- A Little Grace—"Let any one of you who is without sin be the first to throw a stone at her" (John 8:7).

- A Little Inclusion—"Know that the Lord is God. It is he who made us, and we are his; we are his people, the sheep of his pasture" (Psalm 100:3).

- A Little Testimony—"They triumphed over him by the blood of the Lamb and by the word of their testimony" (Revelation 12:11).

- A Little Tradition—"This is a day you are to commemorate; for the generations to come you shall celebrate it as a festival to the Lord—a lasting ordinance" (Exodus 12:14).

- A Little Gesture—"Then Mary took about a pint of pure nard, an expensive perfume; she poured it on Jesus' feet and wiped his feet with her hair. And the house was filled with the fragrance of the perfume" (John 12:3).

- A Little Letter—"You yourselves are our letter, written on our hearts, known and read by everyone. You show that you are a letter from Christ, the result of our ministry, written not with ink but with the Spirit of the living God, not on tablets of stone but on tablets of human hearts" (2 Corinthians 3:2–3).

- A Little Courage—"For the Spirit God gave us does not make us timid, but gives us power, love and self-discipline" (2 Timothy 1:7).

- A Little Thought—"Finally, brothers, whatever is true, whatever is noble, whatever is right, whatever is pure, whatever is lovely, whatever is admirable—if anything is excellent or praiseworthy—think about such things" (Philippians 4:8).

- A Little Clothing—"I needed clothes, and you clothed me" (Matthew 25:36).

- A Little Gratitude—"Let the message of Christ dwell among you richly as you teach and admonish one another with all the wisdom through psalms, hymns, and songs from the Spirit, singing to God with gratitude in your heart. And whatever you do, whether in word or deed, do it all in the name of the Lord Jesus, giving thanks to God the Father through him" (Colossians 3:16–17).

- A Little Encouragement—"Therefore encourage one another and build each other up, just as in fact you are doing" (1 Thessalonians 5:11).

- A Little Story—"Then Philip ran up to the chariot and heard the man reading Isaiah the prophet. 'Do you understand what you are reading?' Philip asked. 'How can I,' he said, 'unless someone explains it to me?' So he invited Philip to come up and sit with him" (Acts 8:30–31).

- A Little Interruption—"When Jesus heard what had happened, he withdrew by boat privately to a solitary place. Hearing of this, the crowds followed him on foot from the towns. When Jesus landed and saw the large crowd, he had compassion on them and healed their sick" (Matthew 14:13–14).

- A Little Perseverance—"Not only so, but we also rejoice in our sufferings, because we know that suffering produces perseverance; perseverance, character; and character, hope" (Romans 5:3–4).

- A Little Seed—"The kingdom of heaven is like a mustard seed, which a man took and planted in his field. Though it is the smallest of all seeds, yet when it grows, it is the largest of the garden plants and becomes a tree, so that the birds of the air come and perch in its branches" (Matthew 13:31–32).

- A Little Kindness—"'May I continue to find favor in your eyes, my lord,' she said. 'You have put me at ease by speaking kindly to your servant—though I do not have the standing of one of your servants'" (Ruth 2:13).

- A Little Look—"Nothing in all creation is hidden from God's sight" (Hebrews 4:13).

- A Little Sacrifice—"Therefore, I urge you, brothers and sisters, in view of God's mercy, to offer your bodies as a living sacrifice, holy and pleasing to God—this is your true and proper worship" (Romans 12:1).

- A Little Forgiveness—"Bear with each other and forgive one another if any of you has a grievance against someone. Forgive as the Lord forgave you" (Colossians 3:13).

- A Little Cup—"Then he took the cup, and when he had given thanks, he gave it to them, and they all drank from it. 'This is the blood of the covenant, which is poured out for many,' he said to them" (Mark 14:23–24).

- A Little Number—"For God so loved the world that he gave his one and only Son, that whoever believes in him shall not perish but have eternal life" (John 3:16).

- A Little Object—"Then the Lord said to him, 'What is that in your hand?'" (Exodus 4:2).

- A Little Vision—"Where there is no vision, the people will perish" (Proverbs 29:18).

- A Little Less—"For it is by grace you have been saved, through faith—and this is not from yourselves, it is the gift of God—not by works, so that no one can boast" (Ephesians 2:8–9).

- A Little by Little—"The Lord your God will drive out those nations before you, little by little. You will not be allowed to eliminate them all at once or the wild animals will multiply around you" (Deuteronomy 7:22).

A Little Flavor

Party Meatballs

Ingredients:
- 2 eggs, beaten
- 1 can (12 ounces) evaporated milk
- 2 cups quick-cooking oats
- 1 cup finely chopped onion
- 2 teaspoons salt
- 2 teaspoons chili powder
- ½ teaspoon garlic powder
- ½ teaspoon pepper
- 3 pounds ground beef

Sauce:
- 2 cups ketchup
- 1 ½ cups packed brown sugar
- ½ cup chopped onion

Instructions:

In a large bowl, combine the first 8 ingredients. Crumble beef over mixture and mix well. Shape into 1-inch balls. Place in 3 greased 13x9x2-inch baking dishes. Combine the sauce ingredients; pour over meatballs. Bake, uncovered, at 325 degrees Fahrenheit for 1 hour or until meat is no longer pink. This recipe should make about 7 dozen meatballs.

Raspberry Jelly

Ingredients:

- 3 pounds raspberries
- 1 ½ cups water
- Sugar
- 2 tablespoons fresh lemon juice
- Coarse salt

Instructions:

Combine fruit and water in a saucepan. Bring to a boil, reduce to a simmer, and cook, partially covered, mashing occasionally with a potato masher, until the fruit is very soft, 10 to 15 minutes. Transfer mixture to a fine sieve set over a heatproof bowl; let drain for 4 hours without pressing on fruit. Strain again through a sieve lined with damp cheesecloth. Measure juice; you will have 3 to 4 cups.

In a large, heavy-bottomed pot, bring juice to a boil. Add ¾ cup sugar for each cup of juice. Add lemon juice and ¼ teaspoon salt. Return to a boil and cook, stirring frequently for 8 to 12 minutes. To test if jelly is done, dip a large metal spoon in, lift it horizontally above the pot, and let the mixture drip back in. Jelly is done when the mixture has thickened slightly and drops of the mixture slide together off the spoon in a sheet. (Temperature should register 221 degrees Fahrenheit on a candy thermometer.) Skim foam from the top.

Ladle jelly into clean containers, leaving ¾ inch of headroom. Let cool completely. Cover, label, and refrigerate for up to 1 month or freeze for up to 1 year.

Crepes

Ingredients:

- 1 cup unbleached all-purpose flour
- 1 tablespoon granulated sugar
- ¼ teaspoon kosher salt
- 1 ½ cups whole milk, room temperature
- 4 large eggs, room temperature
- 3 tablespoons unsalted butter, melted, plus more for brushing

Instructions:

In a blender, puree flour, sugar, salt, milk, eggs, and butter until smooth, about 30 seconds. Refrigerate for 30 minutes or up to 1 day; stir for a few seconds before using. Heat an 8-inch nonstick skillet over medium heat. Lightly coat with butter. Quickly pour ¼ cup batter into the center of the skillet, tilting and swirling the pan until the batter evenly coats the bottom. Cook until crepe is golden in places on bottom and edges begin to lift from pan, 1 to 1 ½ minutes. Lift one edge of the crepe with an offset spatula, then use your fingers to gently flip the crepe. Cook on the second side until just set and golden in places on the bottom, about 45 seconds. Slide crepe onto a paper towel–lined plate. Repeat with remaining batter, coating pan with more butter as needed and stacking crepes directly on top of one another. Let cool to room temperature before using, wrapping leftovers in plastic wrap and refrigerating for up to 5 days or freezing up to 1 month.

Nutmeg Log Cookies

Ingredients:
- 1 cup butter, softened
- ¾ cup sugar
- 1 large egg, room temperature
- 2 teaspoons rum extract
- 2 ½ cups all-purpose flour
- 1 ¼ teaspoons ground nutmeg
- Dash salt

Frosting:
- ¼ cup butter, softened
- 3 cups confectioner's sugar
- 1 ½ to 2 teaspoons rum extract
- 2 to 3 tablespoons 2% milk
- Ground nutmeg

Instructions:
In a large bowl, cream butter and sugar until light and fluffy, 5 to 7 minutes. Beat in egg and rum extract. Combine the flour, nutmeg, and salt; gradually add to the creamed mixture, and mix well. Divide dough into 3 portions. Roll each portion into ¾-inch thick logs; chill until firm, about 30 minutes. Cut into 2-inch pieces. Place on ungreased baking sheets; flatten slightly. Bake at 350 degrees Fahrenheit for 12 to 16 minutes or until bottoms are lightly browned. Cool for 2 minutes before removing to wire racks to cool completely.

For frosting, in a large bowl, beat butter until fluffy. Beat in the confectioner's sugar, rum extract, and enough milk to achieve desired consistency. Frost cookies. Press down with tines of a fork, making lines in frosting to simulate tree bark. Sprinkle with nutmeg. This recipe should make around 3 dozen cookies.

Snickerdoodle Cookies

Ingredients:
- 1 cup unsalted butter, softened
- 1 ½ cups sugar
- 2 large eggs
- 2 teaspoons vanilla
- 2 ¾ cups flour
- 1 ½ teaspoons cream of tartar
- ½ teaspoon baking soda
- 1 teaspoon salt

Cinnamon-Sugar Mixture:
- ¼ cup sugar
- 1 ½ tablespoons cinnamon

Instructions:
Preheat the oven to 350 degrees Fahrenheit. In a large mixing bowl, cream butter and sugar for 4 to 5 minutes until light and fluffy. Scrape the sides of the bowl, and add the eggs and vanilla. Cream for 1 to 2 minutes longer. Stir in flour, cream of tartar, baking soda, and salt, just until combined. In a small bowl, stir together sugar and cinnamon.

If time allows, wrap the dough, and let it refrigerate for 20 to 30 minutes. Roll into small balls until round and smooth. Drop into the cinnamon-sugar mixture, and coat well. Using a spoon, coat for a second time, ensuring the cookie balls are completely covered. To make flatter snickerdoodles, press down in the center of the ball before placing in the oven. This helps to keep them from puffing up in the middle. Place on a parchment paper–lined baking sheet. Bake for 9 to 11 minutes. Let cool for several minutes on a baking sheet before removing from the pan. This recipe should make around 2 dozen cookies.

Nighty Night Cookies

Ingredients:

- 2 egg whites
- ⅔ cup sugar
- 6 ounces chocolate chips

Instructions:

Preheat the oven to 350 degrees Fahrenheit. Beat egg whites until stiff. Gradually add ⅔ cup sugar, beating until stiff. Stir in chocolate chips. Drop by teaspoon on a foil-lined cookie sheet. Place in the oven. Close the door, turn off the oven, and leave them in the oven all night. *Do not peek.*

Lemon Poppy Seed Bundt Cake

Ingredients:

Lemon Poppy Seed Bundt Cake:

- 2 ¾ cups all-purpose flour, spooned and leveled
- 1 teaspoon baking powder
- ½ teaspoon baking soda

- 1 teaspoon salt
- 3 tablespoons poppy seeds
- ¾ cup unsalted butter, softened
- 2 cups granulated sugar
- 4 large eggs, room temperature
- 2 teaspoons vanilla extract
- ⅓ cup fresh lemon juice
- 2 tablespoons lemon zest
- ¼ cup canola or vegetable oil
- 1 cup sour cream
- Cooking spray

Lemon Glaze:
- 1 cup confectioner's sugar
- 2 to 3 tablespoons fresh lemon juice (or as needed to thin out the glaze)

Instructions:

Preheat the oven to 350 degrees Fahrenheit. In a large mixing bowl, whisk together the flour, baking powder, baking soda, salt, and poppy seeds. Set aside.

In the bowl of a stand mixer fitted with the paddle attachment, or a large mixing bowl using a handheld mixer, beat the butter and sugar until light and fluffy. Mix in the eggs one at a time, then mix in the vanilla. Slowly mix in the lemon juice, lemon zest, and oil. Alternate mixing the flour mixture and the sour cream into the wet ingredients, starting with the flour and ending with the flour. Mix until just combined.

Spray a 10-inch Bundt pan well with nonstick cooking spray. Pour the batter into the prepared Bundt pan and evenly spread it around.

Bake at 350 degrees for 45 to 55 minutes or until a toothpick inserted into the cake comes out clean. Cover loosely with foil if needed for the last 5 to 10 minutes of baking to prevent excess browning. Remove from the oven, and cool in the pan on a wire rack for 30 minutes. Then invert the cake onto a wire rack to finish cooling.

To make the glaze, add the confectioner's sugar and lemon juice to a small mixing bowl, and mix until fully combined. Once the cake has cooled, place a piece of foil under the wire rack to catch any glaze that falls off. Pour the lemon glaze evenly over the cake, and allow to harden for about 10 to 15 minutes. Slice and enjoy!

Pan size: If you don't have a Bundt pan, you can also make this recipe in two 8x8-inch cake pans.

Storage instructions: Store the cake in an airtight container at room temperature for up to five days. Unglazed cake can be frozen for up to 3 months and thawed to room temperature before serving.

A Little Acknowledgment

I am forever indebted to the people who made this devotional a reality. A special thanks to the Blythe Daniel Agency for being the first to believe in me as a writer. Blythe, your wisdom and support are invaluable. I know you care about the message in this book, and I know you care about me.

Thank you to Carlton Garborg and the BroadStreet Publishing team for pursuing this project. I am grateful to be included in your list of authors. I am so appreciative of the expertise of Tim Payne, Nina Rose, Jessica Pollard, and the entire editing team who took my thoughts and words and made them better. I am equally thankful for the marketing team who helped take this message farther than I ever dreamed possible.

Thank you to Julie Harris for encouraging me to begin writing and podcasting. You have been a trusted confidant since the beginning when this reality was just a dream.

Thank you to Carina Alanson for brainstorming and fine-tuning every word you see on these pages. I'm so grateful for your encouragement as an editor and as a friend.

Thank you to Megan Conner, who devoted her time and energy to talking through each idea and every sentence. Your selflessness is inspiring, and your friendship is a gift.

To my She Speaks sisterhood, hope*writers circles, Called Creatives masterminds, and Compel Training support groups, I owe you an extra dose of gratitude for championing me and cheering me on.

To my *The Love Offering* podcast guests, listeners, and social media friends, I'm thankful to be living out my faith alongside you. I believe every interaction with you has mattered.

To my Marco Polo and Voxer friends, even though we live far apart, I hold you very near and dear to my heart.

To my local family and friends, thank you for loving me for who I am and for believing in me before I believed in myself. I am blessed to live life alongside you.

To you, who picked up this book. I am humbled. I pray it helps you believe in your God-given significance and his purpose for you right where you are.

And to God. None of this would be a reality without him. I give him all of the glory.

A Little about the Author

Rachael was born and raised in a small Kentucky lake town. After she married her college sweetheart, Bryan, she moved him there too. Together, they run a family business and live on a farm with their two children, Will and Kate, and two doodle dogs named Buster and Penny.

Rachael spends her days taking care of their farm and home. When she isn't doing something with or for her family, she loves to get together with friends, cook, take walks, soak in a bath, and read Christian nonfiction.

Her writing and podcasting journey began when she was sitting in church and saw a love offering envelope in the pew in front of her. She sensed the Lord whispering to her heart that we are his love offerings to the world. So Rachael began having conversations with women who were living faithfully and loving the world around them in practical and tangible ways.

Through the conversations she's had and through her own personal experience, Rachael discovered that many of us don't believe our contributions or offerings matter. It is Rachael's hope that this devotional and her ministry can change this narrative, that women will be encouraged and realize their God-given purpose, and that they will believe their lives are significant to his kingdom. In God's hands, small acts done with great love can have an enormous impact.

Rachael would love to hear how you've seen God take your little a long way. Connect with her by visiting rachaelkadams.com, by searching @rachaeladamsauthor on social media, and by tuning in to *The Love Offering* podcast every Tuesday on your favorite listening platform. Be sure to tune into the *A Little Goes a Long Way* episodes that correspond with each devotion!

A Special Little Love Offering for You!

To show her appreciation, Rachael has created the *A Little Goes a Long Way Journal and Conversation Guide* to help you continue this journey on your own, with a friend, or in a group. This journal is meant to be a companion to your devotional reading so you have a space to record your reflections. Then, if you want, you can utilize the prompts to guide your conversations with your group about how everything you are doing is going a long way! Visit rachaelkadams.com/free to receive your gift.